The Science Student's Guide to Dissertations and Research Projects

For a complete listing of all our titles in this area please visit
https://www.bloomsbury.com/uk/academic/study-skills

www.thestudyspace.com – the leading study
skills website

Study Skills

Academic Success
Academic Writing Skills for International Students
Ace Your Exam
Be Well, Learn Well
Becoming a Critical Thinker
The Bloomsbury Student Planner
Brilliant Essays
The Business Student's Phrase Book
Cite Them Right (12th edn)
Critical Thinking and Persuasive Writing for
  Postgraduates
Critical Thinking for Nursing, Health and Social Care
Critical Thinking Skills (3rd edn)
Dissertations and Project Reports
Doing Projects and Reports in Engineering
The Employability Journal
Essentials of Essay Writing
The Exam Skills Handbook (2nd edn)
Get Sorted
The Graduate Career Guidebook (2nd edn)
Great Ways to Learn Anatomy and Physiology
  (2nd edn)
How to Use Your Reading in Your Essays (3rd edn)
How to Write Better Essays (5th edn)
How to Write Your Literature Review
How to Write Your Undergraduate Dissertation
  (3rd edn)
Improve Your Grammar (3rd edn)
Mindfulness for Students
Presentation Skills for Students (3rd edn)
The Principles of Writing in Psychology
Professional Writing (4th edn)
Reading at University
Reflective Writing for Nursing, Health and Social
  Work
The Science Student's Guide to Dissertations and
  Research Projects
Simplify Your Study
Skills for Business and Management
Skills for Success (4th edn)
Smart Thinking
Stand Out from the Crowd
The Student Phrase Book (2nd edn)
The Student's Guide to Writing (3rd edn)
Study Skills for International Postgraduates (2nd edn)
The Study Skills Handbook (5th edn)
Studying in English
Studying Law (4th edn)
The Study Success Journal
Success in Academic Writing (2nd edn)
Teaching Study Skills and Supporting Learning
The Undergraduate Research Handbook (2nd edn)
The Work-Based Learning Student Handbook
  (3rd edn)
Write it Right (2nd edn)
Writing for Biomedical Sciences Students

Writing for Engineers (4th edn)
Writing for Nursing and Midwifery Students
  (3rd edn)
Writing for Science Students (2nd edn)
Writing Skills for Education Students
Writing Skills for Social Work Students
You2Uni: Decide, Prepare, Apply

Pocket Study Skills

14 Days to Exam Success (2nd edn)
Analyzing a Case Study
Brilliant Writing Tips for Students
Completing Your PhD
Doing Research (2nd edn)
Getting Critical (3rd edn)
How to Analyze Data
Managing Stress
Planning Your Dissertation (3rd edn)
Planning Your Essay (3rd edn)
Planning Your PhD
Posters and Presentations
Reading and Making Notes (3rd edn)
Referencing and Understanding Plagiarism (2nd edn)
Reflective Writing (2nd edn)
Report Writing (2nd edn)
Science Study Skills
Studying with Dyslexia (2nd edn)
Success in Groupwork (2nd edn)
Successful Applications
Time Management
Using Feedback to Boost Your Grades
Where's Your Argument? (2nd edn)
Where's Your Evidence?
Writing for University (3rd edn)

50 Ways

50 Ways to Boost Your Employability
50 Ways to Boost Your Grades
50 Ways to Excel at Writing
50 Ways to Manage Stress
50 Ways to Manage Time Effectively
50 Ways to Succeed as an International Student

Research Skills

Authoring a PhD
The Foundations of Research (3rd edn)
Getting Published
Getting to Grips with Doctoral Research
The Good Supervisor (2nd edn)
The Lean PhD
Maximizing the Impacts of Academic Research
PhD by Published Work
The PhD Viva
The PhD Writing Handbook
Planning Your Postgraduate Research
The Postgraduate Research Handbook (2nd edn)
The Postgraduate's Guide to Research Ethics
The Professional Doctorate
Structuring Your Research Thesis

The *Science* Student's Guide to Dissertations and Research Projects

Jessica Bownes

BLOOMSBURY ACADEMIC
LONDON • NEW YORK • OXFORD • NEW DELHI • SYDNEY

BLOOMSBURY ACADEMIC
Bloomsbury Publishing Plc
50 Bedford Square, London, WC1B 3DP, UK
1385 Broadway, New York, NY 10018, USA
29 Earlsfort Terrace, Dublin 2, Ireland

BLOOMSBURY, BLOOMSBURY ACADEMIC and the Diana logo
are trademarks of Bloomsbury Publishing Plc

First published in Great Britain 2023

A catalogue record for this book is available from the British Library.

Library of Congress Cataloging-in-Publication Data
Names: Bownes, Jessica, author.
Title: The science student's guide to dissertations and research projects / Jessica Bownes.
Description: London ; New York, NY : Bloomsbury Academic, 2023. |
Series: Bloomsbury study skills | Includes bibliographical references and index. |
Summary: "The Science Student's Guide to Dissertations and Research
Projects guides students through the entire process of working on a dissertation, from the early
but crucial planning stages, through to undertaking practical work and collecting data, researching
literature, and writing up one's findings. Each chapter includes lists, step-by-step guides and plenty of
examples, making it practical and easy-to-follow. The book also provides strategies for when things go
wrong with advice on managing stress, procrastination and unexpected data"– Provided by publisher.
Identifiers: LCCN 2022039199 | ISBN 9781350323681 (paperback) | ISBN 9781350323841 (pdf)
| ISBN 9781350323834 (epub) | ISBN 9781350323827
Subjects: LCSH: Dissertations, Academic–Authorship. | Dissertations, Academic–Style manuals. |
Academic writing–Handbooks, manuals, etc. | Science–Study and teaching
(Higher)–Handbooks, manuals, etc.
Classification: LCC LB2369 .B685 2023 | DDC 808.06/6378–dc23/eng/20221219
LC record available at https://lccn.loc.gov/2022039199

ISBN: PB: 978-1-3503-2368-1
         ePDF: 978-1-3503-2384-1
         eBook: 978-1-3503-2383-4

Series: Bloomsbury Study Skills

Typeset by Integra Software Services Pvt. Ltd.
Printed and bound in Great Britain

To find out more about our authors and books visit www.bloomsbury.com
and sign up for our newsletters.

To my brother. Oh hi, Jon!

Contents

List of figures

List of tables

Introduction

In my job, I teach and give academic advice to students across many different science disciplines. I am the Learning Adviser for around eight thousand students, so I am asked a lot of questions about how to conduct and write about scientific research. It's remarkable how similar the questions are from very different subjects. From Chemistry to Geography, Psychology to Physics, students share the same uncertainty and curiosity about their reports and dissertations. This book takes those questions and distils my advice into one place.

Most of the students I see are undertaking research at their current level of study for the first time. Undergraduates may have never had the opportunity to complete this sort of work and postgraduates want to know how to improve their research skills to meet new expectations. I speak to students who feel daunted about working with a supervisor for the first time: what does that new working relationship look like? Many are overwhelmed by the sheer volume and perceived complexity of the academic literature. Sifting through the work on their topic and critically evaluating what they find can be challenging. And then there's the writing. Because of the nature of science degrees, lots of students don't write their first lengthy piece of science writing until the later years of their course. Unlike Arts students, who practise and refine their writing style from day one, Science students are more likely to be tested on their knowledge of their subject via multiple choice tests, short lab reports and exams. Lots of scientists enjoy the practical side to their subject but are less sure about writing up their results. In a dissertation or a research report, however, it's the writing that usually carries the most marks, just as the written article in the academic literature is viewed and discussed much more than the actual lab or field work.

Knowing all of these questions you might have as a scientific researcher, this book guides you through each stage of your research, from deciding a topic to handing in. There is a particular emphasis on writing up your research report because this is the most important aspect of your work when it comes to your feedback and grades. My hope is that this book helps you to enjoy your research a little bit more. Research should be interesting and exciting (although there will be times when you question this, such as when you are in your third hour of pipetting colourless liquid or counting a particular species of insect in a square metre). There's nothing quite like when you finally get your data and, even better, it makes sense! Your upcoming project will give you a flavour of what it will be like if you decide to make a career in scientific research. This book will help you get the most out of that experience.

What is a dissertation and a research report in STEM?

The words 'dissertation' and 'report' are used interchangeably in this book because they are essentially the same type of work – they are the written component of an academic research project. It is common to be required to complete one or more short research projects before undertaking your dissertation. These shorter reports are an opportunity to practise your research skills and get feedback on a lower stakes assessment before you complete a larger and more high-stakes project. Because of this, the advice in this book applies to any length of research report in a sciences subject and will be particularly useful if your project involves collecting and analysing quantitative data in the lab or in the field.

By completing your research project, you will use and develop a whole host of different academic and professional skills that will be relevant to your chosen career path. You will be required to analyse a range of different sources, make independent decisions about the direction of your research, manage your time effectively, motivate yourself and solve any problems you encounter along the way – this book has information on how to best approach all of these aspects of research. By definition, academic research should reveal something new in your subject, but the extent to how novel your research has to be is dictated by the individual assessment you are undertaking so make sure you are clear about this before you begin any work on your project.

Undergraduate vs. postgraduate dissertations

Although this book is suitable for both undergraduate and postgraduate taught students who are completing research in a science-based subject, it is important to note the differences in expectations between the two levels of study so that you can apply the advice here accordingly. The main research tasks and structure of a research report in an undergraduate and a postgraduate course are largely the same. There are some differences in the expectation of academic standards, since institutions acknowledge that your undergraduate dissertation is probably your first attempt at a large piece of research, whereas a postgraduate course assumes some prior experience and therefore demands more in terms of quality. Of course, this means that whatever level you are studying at, you should approach your research with the intentions of producing your best standard of work since most dissertations carry a large weighting of marks in a course and can often decide the final outcome of your degree.

If you are a postgraduate student, bear in mind that expectations of academic standard will be justifiably higher than in your undergraduate degree. For your final research project, this means that your report might be around 50 per cent longer in word count than your undergraduate dissertation, and a longer report means more complexity and depth of research is expected. As well as a longer finished product, the practical side of your research might look very different to any prior experiences you've had. Undergraduate research tends to be more directed by supervisors, with research questions and methodology already designed for you. Postgraduate research is usually much more independent, given that many students who are undertaking master's courses are preparing for PhD study where all the research is self-directed. In addition to more self-direction, postgraduate dissertations tend to include more original research, with a greater expectation that the result will contribute something tangible to the subject you are studying. Novel research comes with more unknowns, and more chances to exercise your problem-solving skills to produce good-quality results. Thankfully, although postgraduate study is often complex, it also involves working more closely with your supervisor than you might have done for your previous degree, so access to advice and support is easier and more frequent.

How to use this book

The advice in this book can be applied to reports and dissertations in most STEM subjects, but will be particularly useful if your project involves collecting and analysing quantitative data in the lab or in the field. This book can be used flexibly, and doesn't need to be read from cover to cover. We advise that you initially take a look through the chapter descriptions below and identify any topics that you'd like to know more about (e.g. working with your supervisor and planning your time). Read through these chapters first and then keep this book handy to refer to as you progress through your research; some of the chapters may be particularly useful to take in later on in your project (e.g. editing and proofreading), so make a note to read these later instead of right at the beginning of your research. This approach, incidentally, is the most effective way for other textbooks and handbooks in your studies, so don't ever read a textbook from beginning to end unless specifically instructed by a tutor!

What is in this book?

The chapters in this book include lists and step-by-step guides where possible to make finding and reading information quick and easy. Examples from a variety of STEM subjects have been used throughout to help you apply the advice to your own work. Use the list below to identify particularly useful content that you might want to read first.

There are ten chapters to this book (including this one). Following this introduction, you will find:

Chapter 2, Using the marking criteria to get the best grade possible, shows you how to use the marking criteria for the assessment you're working on to plan and check your work.

Chapter 3, Working with your supervisor, discusses how to navigate and get the most out of the student–supervisor relationship. If you have never worked with a supervisor before, this chapter will be very useful in learning the obligations and expectations of both parties.

Chapter 4, Planning your work, contains information about time management, maintaining motivation and overcoming potential setbacks during your project. There are several tools in this chapter that will help you to plan and structure the practical and written elements of your research.

Chapter 5, Collecting your data, guides you through the key considerations when completing the practical portion of your research with an emphasis on working ethically and maintaining good academic practice so that your data is credible.

Chapter 6, Finding and analysing the literature, explains the various sources of academic literature, how to organize what you find and how to critically analyse the papers that will be useful in your work.

Chapter 7, Using evidence in your dissertation, discusses the key evidence that you will use in your research and how to incorporate evidence into your writing. Academic literature, novel data (i.e. the data you collect for your project), statistical evidence and visual evidence are all discussed.

Chapter 8, Writing a science dissertation, is a comprehensive guide to the content and structure of a science research report. By the end of this chapter, you will have a good understanding of what a good-quality report looks like.

Chapter 9, Avoiding plagiarism in your research, addresses the often-complex topic of referencing and plagiarism. This chapter will help you to recognize what plagiarism is and, crucially, will help you understand how to properly reference your sources so that you don't accidentally plagiarize.

Chapter 10, Editing and proofreading, details the tasks involved in correcting and refining your writing. The chapter describes a five-stage process that will result in a polished and professional report.

At the back of the book is a glossary of terms. Refer to the glossary if you ever come across an unfamiliar term in the book.

Using the marking criteria to get the best grade possible

Introduction

The marker who grades your research report or dissertation will follow marking guidelines that are specific to your assessment. These guidelines break down the criteria which must be fulfilled by a student to achieve each grade, from a fail to a first-class grade. It is a good idea to familiarize yourself with these criteria before you begin any work on your project (either practical or written) so that you can use it to your advantage while you're working over the next few weeks or months. After all, if you know how your report will be marked, you will know what your lecturer is looking for in a good-quality report. This chapter will show you how to make the most of the marking scheme, and how to use it to begin planning your research.

Topics in this chapter include:

- How your tutors mark your work
- Using the marking scheme to your advantage
- How to conduct a self-evaluation to get the best mark in your research.

How do lecturers use the marking scheme?

A note about planning and procrastination

One pitfall to avoid when planning your research is the temptation to use exercises such as self-evaluations as a means of procrastination. Planning-based procrastination is dangerous because it feels beneficial and seems different to procrastination activities that outright avoid the larger task at hand (scrolling through social media, for example). Remember, though, that both types of procrastination won't actually get the job done.

The self-evaluation stage described in this chapter is a very useful one that will help you to go into your research project feeling informed and prepared. Bear in mind, though, that this stage is a short and temporary part of your dissertation. You should work through the self-evaluation quickly, otherwise you will only delay the implementation of your ideas. If you find yourself drafting and redrafting your plan, or if your evaluation is taking longer than an afternoon, take this as your cue to leave it where it is and move on. You might come back to it at a later stage and be more productive.

Procrastination can strike at any point in the planning, practical or writing stages of your research project. It is an inevitable part of undertaking any large body of work. Chapter 4 in this book will help you to be able to recognize and mitigate the effects of procrastination.

Each individual assessment that you complete at university is designed alongside its own marking scheme. Each exam, essay, presentation and report that you submit is marked according to these guidelines. This ensures that the marking process is fair and consistent across students and between academic years. The marking criteria will be separated into several different categories, and a descriptor will be attributed to each category for every one of the grades that are available. The resulting criteria will look something like the simplified example below (see Table 1), but the layout of different criteria can vary between courses, subjects and universities. The marking scheme for your report will be based upon the intended learning outcomes (ILOs) for your course. These are usually defined in a course handbook, and specify the various skills and knowledge that a student should be able to demonstrate upon the completion of a module. Example ILOs for a research project are shown below, but (again) these will vary between different subjects.

Example intended learning outcomes

1. The ability to find and synthesize academic literature to enable the critical analysis of key issues and concepts in the chosen topic.
2. To demonstrate understanding of the key considerations that should be taken into account when dealing with novel data.
3. The ability to critically evaluate novel data and the academic literature.
4. The ability to use primary data and the published literature to produce clear findings that answer a defined research question.

Degree classification	Mark range (%)	Grade (A–E)	Grade descriptors				
			Quality of academic writing	Structure of report	Use of evidence	Presentation and interpretation of data
First (undergraduate) or Distinction (postgraduate)	100–70	A	Writing is clear, concise and objective. The student is able to articulate complicated scientific concepts with adequate amounts of detail, using understandable language.	The structure is logical and professional, making good use of headings and subheadings. Each chapter is laid out in a way that shows logical progression of the academic argument.	Excellent use of scientific evidence (both original and published) to back up the student's claims. The literature is reviewed in depth, presenting a balanced academic view on the subject.	Data are clearly explained in figures, tables and text. Figures and tables have all necessary components. The student is aware of the limitations of their data and the interpretation is unbiased.
2:1 (undergraduate) or Merit (postgraduate)	69–60	B	Writing is, on the whole clear, concise and objective. There are minor issues of clarity, but these are infrequent and do not cloud the student's argument.	The overall structure is logical and professional. The structure within the chapters could be optimized to better serve the academic argument.	A wide range of evidence is used to back up claims. The critical analysis is strong, unbiased and largely well-balanced.	Good use of figures and tables to present data, even though there are minor components missing. Student's discussion of data is full and unbiased.

Table 1 Example of marking criteria for a dissertation or report in a science-based subject

2:2 (undergraduate) or Pass (postgraduate)	59–50	C	Writing is mostly clear and objective. Concision is an issue: the student doesn't make full use of the conventions of scientific writing to convey arguments concisely.	The student has considered the structure of the report, but this could be improved. The academic argument presented within the chapters is not always clear.	Some evidence has been presented to back up claims, but this could be more extensive. Critical analysis has been demonstrated but tends to be slightly one sided.	Figures and tables are present and largely clear. Captions for each should be clearer and more specific. The student discusses their data well, but without consideration of the limitations.
Third (undergraduate) or Fail (postgraduate)	49–40	D	The meaning of the writing is clear, but is protracted and presented in an informal, journalistic tone.	While the report is structured into distinct chapters effectively. The within-text structure is poor.	A limited amount of evidence has been cited and the consideration of the literature is not well connected to the student's own work.	There are figures and tables in the report, but they are not adequately discussed in the text. The discussion of data lacks depth.
Fail	39–0	E–H	The quality of the writing is poor. The student doesn't follow appropriate scientific convention and the argument is obscured by poor grammar.	The report is incorrectly structured or has no defined headings/subheadings. The arguments are also not well structured within the text.	There are some citations, but they aren't generally from credible sources. The range of evidence is poor and critical analysis is basic.	While figures and table are used, the misuse of plot types and necessary components makes the data unclear. Interpretation is minimal.

Table 1 (Continued)

Using the intended learning outcomes and the grade descriptors in the marking scheme, a marker will decide which grade band a student's report fits best into. There will be instances where a report might seem to sit somewhere in between grades, or may have attained some, but not all, of the different criteria within a grade. In this case, the marker will assign the grade that matches the report the closest. This is why every UK university uses a second-marking system when grading assignments, whereby a proportion of students' work is independently marked by a second lecturer, to ensure consistency between markers and fairness towards every student. Third markers may be employed where markers cannot agree on a single grade, and external markers may be used to ensure that grades are standardized between institutions.

How can students use the marking scheme?

You can (and should) familiarize yourself with the marking scheme of each assignment before you begin any work. There may be distinct schemes for the practical parts and written parts of your project – be sure that you have the full information. For the purposes of fairness and transparency, the marking scheme should be made available to students in advance of the assessment being set. You're most likely to find your marking scheme in a course handbook or on your Virtual Learning Environment (Moodle, Blackboard, etc.). If you're unable to find the marking scheme, your lecturer or supervisor should be able to point you in the right direction. It's important not only that you read your marking scheme, but that you fully understand it. Grade descriptors may contain unfamiliar pedagogical terms, and it will be difficult to implement the marking scheme in your project if you don't understand these. A glossary of common terms that are used in grade descriptors for science research projects is shown opposite. See also Chapter 11 of this book for a glossary of terms that are commonly used in the course of academic research.

Exercise 1: Self-evaluation

Once you have located and understood the marking criteria for your specific research project, you should have a fair understanding of what your project should look like, and you can begin linking your work to the criteria using the simple two-step mapping exercise below.

Term	Definition
Adduce evidence	To present evidence in support of a claim.
Application of scientific conventions	Presenting your research according to the defined rules of writing and practice in your particular subject. See Chapters 5 and 8 for an explanation of common conventions in academic science.
Clear hypothesis	The theory or assumption that what you are testing in your research is clearly stated, reasonable and backed up with evidence.
Critical analysis/evaluation	The expression of academic opinion which is balanced (considered from all angles), unbiased and backed up by external evidence.
Delimitation of the project	The boundaries or scope of the research.
Demonstration of implications	To show how the findings of your research affect your field and/or the wider world.
Engagement with literature	Writing about published research (usually from journal articles).
Independent thought	Expressing your own ideas about research (both yours and other people's).
Integration of knowledge	Combining the findings of your study with existing research/information.
Logical progression of argument	Connecting ideas in a way that leads the reader to a sensible conclusion.
Methodological innovation	The production of a new or adapted research method.
Product	The novel artefact that has resulted from your research. This could be either a physical artefact (e.g. a new software programme) or a theoretical product (e.g. the addition of knowledge in your field).
Reflection on research/ literature	Discussing research (yours or someone else's) in hindsight, either after completing the practical study or reading the available, relevant journal articles.
Synthesis of information/ literature	Combining lots of information or ideas from research to form a conclusion.
Unbiased discussion	The impartial consideration of all the available evidence.
Validity of research	How reliable and credible your work is. Validity is achieved through the application of scientific conventions to investigate a legitimate problem.

Table 2   Grade descriptor glossary

Step 1: Decide on your target grade

Research shows us that self-defined target-setting is beneficial to academic performance (Martin and Elliot 2016). The grade that you aim for in your project does not have to be the top one! While it's perfectly reasonable to hope for the top grade, this may not be appropriate for everyone. Maybe, like many students, you're hoping for a 2:1 in your degree, in which case a grade B or mark of 60 per cent would be your target. You could be undertaking a master's degree to secure a promotion at work, in which case a grade C or mark of 50 per cent might be your aim. It is sensible to think about your target grade in terms of your own abilities (demonstrated by your assessment grades in your degree to date) and your aspirations. You should read each grade descriptor in the marking criteria when deciding on your target grade. If you can't decide between two grades, stretch yourself and aim for the greater of the two. Be realistic, but don't be afraid to give yourself a challenge to work towards.

Step 2: Do a self-evaluation

Self-evaluation will allow you to identify your current abilities in relation to the grade you're aiming for and, crucially, those skills that you will need to work on to achieve your goal. Self-evaluation is one of the tools that you should regularly employ throughout your degree to identify your strengths and areas for improvement. The diagram below describes the process of self-evaluation. It should take no longer than an hour or so to complete.

Map your skills
- For your chosen target grade, read through each of the grade descriptors and highlight the knowledge and skills that you are most confident in demonstrating.
- Think (or look) back at previous feedback from assessments to find other examples of your academic strengths.

Identify skills gaps
- Identify any descriptors that describe skills that you're not so confident in or are not looking forward to doing in your research.
- Check feedback for areas of improvement that lecturers have highlighted and consider whether you've already addressed these or are still working on them.

Make a plan
- Think about how you will demonstrate your academic strengths as you work through your research.
- Make a short and achievable plan for addressing your identified weaknesses. This plan could include attending academic development workshops, asking for advice from your supervisor or looking up online resources to help you improve.

Figure 1   A self-evaluation exercise to complete before you begin your research

How often should I self-evaluate?

You should perform a self-evaluation before you undertake any large research project or dissertation to identify your strengths and weaknesses before you start. Successful students also self-evaluate regularly throughout the course of the academic year. Checking in with your progress twice a semester or once per term will help you to hone your academic skills. Self-evaluation is also a good practice to take forward into your post-university life to support your continuous professional development in your chosen career.

Next steps

	Obtain your marking criteria
	Take the time to read and understand the criteria
	Perform a self-evaluation
	Create a plan to upskill
	Think about how you will use the marking scheme as you progress through your project

Working with your supervisor

Introduction

You will probably be asked to work with a supervisor for the duration of your dissertation or research project. This will be an academic member of staff in your department who will have some expertise in your topic. It may be the first time that you have worked in this type of dynamic – it is very different to a typical student–lecturer relationship; this chapter will help you to navigate this relationship by explaining the roles involved and the expectations of each person. A good supervisor–researcher relationship will result in a much more productive and successful research project.

Topics in this chapter include:

- Choosing and approaching a potential supervisor
- Building a good working relationship with your supervisor
- Adapting to different supervision styles
- Accessing support apart from your supervisor.

Why do you work with a supervisor?

There are a few reasons why you will have been asked to work with a supervisor. Firstly, it is very likely that this is the first time you are undertaking a significant research project or (if you are doing your master's dissertation) it is the first time that you are working at your current academic level. Your project is also likely to contribute significantly to the way that your final degree result is calculated – for many institutions, you are required to pass your dissertation or final research project to graduate with an honours degree or MSc, and the work itself is usually worth a high number of course credits. Given the value of your dissertation to your degree, you will probably want to access all of the help and support available to you. Your supervisor will be able to provide you with specialist and often personalized advice about how to navigate your research project.

In addition to increasing the likelihood of success in your project, working with a supervisor will give you valuable experience and insight into what it's like to work as a professional academic researcher. PhD students and postdoctoral researchers all work with a supervisor under a very similar dynamic to that you'll experience during your dissertation. Even if you are not considering an academic career, you'll get a sense of what it will be like to take ownership of projects and report back to a manager – these are the sorts of transferable skills that employers look for in their prospective candidates.

Who is your supervisor?

Choosing your supervisor

Some programmes allow or require you to approach a staff member in your department to ask them to supervise you and your project. If this is the case for you, you have the advantage of being able to tailor your dissertation experience to suit your wants and needs. When considering whom to approach as a potential supervisor, there are a few things you should consider:

Ask yourself three questions when considering a supervisor:

1. What topics are you interested to know more about?
2. Are there any topics that are closely connected to your post-university career?
3. What topics have you studied so far that you are particularly adept at?

Notice that the initial considerations when choosing a supervisor are related to the subject of your research rather than the person you'll work with. This is because you'll get very little benefit from working with a supervisor that you get on with on a project that you're not invested in – you'll definitely spend more time with your dissertation than your supervisor! Have a look through your previous years' course materials when considering research topics. It's best if you choose something that staff in your department have expertise in, and lecturers usually teach the topics that they are interested in.

You don't need to have a fully formed research plan to approach a supervisor – a topic of interest and a couple of avenues of investigation are a good stage to get to. Once you have an idea of what you'd like to research, you can then identify an academic who is also interested in that topic. You might consider the lecturer whose class got you interested in the subject area, but widen your search to other staff in your subject department to find the right fit for you. Most Higher Education institutions have a list of staff by department on their website; these lists usually include staff contact details and research interests – mine these lists for staff who share your academic interests.

Dear Dr Liang,

I'm a final year Biology student in the department of Life Sciences and I'm due to complete my honours project this year. I am interested in researching craniofacial growth and development and believe that you would be a good fit as a supervisor for my project due to our shared research interests and your expertise in the area.

If you are accepting new dissertation students this academic year, I'd be very grateful for a meeting with you to discuss my ideas for a research project. I am on campus on Mondays, Thursdays and Fridays at the moment.

Best wishes,
Sarah Gethin
Student number: 0208497

Once you've identified a good academic fit and you're happy that you'd get on professionally with that person, it's time to broach the subject with your prospective supervisor. Timing is important when choosing a dissertation supervisor; there may be several students who also want to work with your preferred staff member, so don't delay with reaching out. See the email template below for an idea of how to word your request in a professional manner.

The above email follows the template:

Appropriate greeting,
[Introduce yourself and your degree subject] [Indication of research interest that links with their own]
[Request for a meeting] [Indication of availability]
Formal close

A timely and professional email request should, for the majority, secure you a meeting to discuss your dissertation. Sometimes, however, your request might be declined because they are either not taking on any more students or they believe that your ideas are a better fit with another member of staff; in this case, it is perfectly acceptable to ask them to recommend an alternative potential supervisor for you to contact. Once you have secured a meeting, it pays to go prepared. Do a bit of reading around your topic of interest to refresh your memory. You could take a look at relevant recent publications (see Chapter 6 for a guide on searching for literature) to get an idea of current questions and problems in your subject. It is also worth looking up any recent publications that your prospective supervisor has written so that you can confidently talk about any shared interests.

If you didn't choose your supervisor ...

Many degree programme don't require you to approach your supervisor yourself, and instead, you will be asked to pick from a list of projects with the supervisors pre-assigned, or to define your research questions and preferred method to which a supervisor will be matched for you. If this is the case for you, you will be able to focus in on the type of project that you want to undertake, more than on the person who will supervise you. There may be one project on the list that jumps out at you as 'your' dissertation. If this is the case then make sure that you get in quick with your request to undertake that particular project. If you are wavering between a few options, you can ask yourself the same three questions listed in the previous section, and make your decision based on the project that closely matches your interests, career aspirations and abilities. When choosing a research project from a list, it can be helpful to rank your preferred three titles; this means that you already have a viable second option if your preferred project is allocated to someone else. The advantage of pre-assigned supervisors is that you don't have to worry about approaching staff with a supervision request (though this is useful experience if you wish to pursue an academic career after your degree).

The student–supervisor relationship

The student–supervisor relationship is possibly a new professional dynamic for you. It helps to know what to expect and what is expected from you. Above all, though, remember that the professional relationship that you cultivate with your supervisor is part of your learning experience; you are not expected to know the intricacies of the academic world and your supervisor will understand that you don't have a wealth of experience to draw from.

The role of a supervisor

The role of a dissertation supervisor is to guide you through your project. The word 'guide' is carefully chosen, as their role is to advise you, but not necessarily to teach you. Your supervisor will have many years of experience in conducting their own research, so be ready to tap that experience to your advantage. In addition to research experience, they will have a wealth of subject knowledge and will probably be experts in their field, so ask them for help with your topic as well as the management of your research.

Ultimately, though, your research belongs to you, so you are responsible for its direction and your supervisor will provide advice: they will tell you where to find answers more often than they will give you answers. Just as different lecturers have different teaching styles, there may be different approaches to supervision as well. Your supervisor may be quite 'hands on', expecting regular meetings and updates. They may provide feedback on your writing or a sample of your writing. Or they may be more distant: meeting with you a couple of times throughout your project. There are advantages to both approaches to supervision and, while many students would prefer the more 'hands-on' approach, having the experience of making your own decisions about your work can be empowering and beneficial. Remember as well that, no matter what 'style' of supervisor you get, you should always contact them when you have a real problem related to your research and you can expect a timely response and some support.

As well as different levels of involvement in your project, supervisors may have different ways of dealing with contact time. Supervisors may communicate exclusively via email, they may invite you to meetings or they may conduct group meetings that include all of their supervisees. Group meetings are particularly useful as you are able to discuss your project and get feedback from your peers as well as a member of staff, but they require the most preparation to ensure you get the most out of your time.

While it pays to be aware of your supervisor's 'style' so that you can get the most benefit out of working with them, don't let this be a factor when choosing whom to work with. Every approach has its strengths and weaknesses and it is up to you as a student to work the strengths to your advantage.

Supervision style	Most likely to say …	Strength	Weakness	How do you get the most out of this supervisor?
Autocratic Gives you tasks to complete rather than suggestions of things to do. This supervisor may be pushed for time and feel it's quicker to give you instructions rather than guidance.	'Your research questions are …'	There are clear expectations and boundaries from the start.	You will probably feel unheard if you disagree with them.	Don't be afraid to ask 'why?' This supervisor will be very clear on the 'what', but less so on the 'why'. If their approach is the best, they will be able to tell you why. If it's not, asking 'why?' will reveal that a different approach may work better.
Hand-holder Helps by doing, rather than advising. This supervisor really wants you to do well and is keen to support.	'Let me do that for you!'	Confidence building for inexperienced researchers.	There's a risk that you don't feel ownership of your research.	Direct this supervisor's keenness to help. Be open about what you are confident with and what you would appreciate help with.
Open-door supervisor This supervisor is supportive but will wait for you to come to them instead of proactively supervising you.	Not a lot … until you ask.	Your research is your own. This supervisor encourages independence and problem solving.	You may feel undirected at times. This style isn't beneficial to those who appreciate structure.	Be proactive with this supervisor. If you need something, no matter how small, ask for it!
Micro-manager The opposite to the open-door supervisor, the micro-manager will be very observant and hands-on.	'Where are you with your chapter?'	People who struggle to self-motivate will benefit as you will be kept accountable.	You might feel pressured by the regular request for updates.	Tell them if their micro-management becomes stressful or overwhelming. They have good intentions and think they are helping!
Collaborative It feels much more like you're working with this supervisor, than for them. They are open to (and expect) your input on your project and will offer the same.	'Let's see if we can find out more about …'	You will feel supported but also that you have a voice in your research.	May worry about letting them down because of the teamwork dynamic with the collaborator.	Ask for help with additional research opportunities, such as conferences and publishing papers.

Table 3 The strengths and weaknesses of different supervision styles

Working with multiple supervisors

You may find that you are required to work with two or more supervisors during your project. This student–supervisor relationship also has its strengths and weaknesses. An obvious strength to working with more than one academic is the increased access to knowledge and support. Indeed, you should consider this point carefully if you are choosing your own supervisors: it often helps to approach academics who have different specializations related to your project to make the most of having multiple supervisors. Communication, however, becomes more complicated with more people involved in your work, and you'll need to consider how you'll make sure that everyone is up to date with your progress.

Include your supervisors

You will communicate with many more people than just your supervisor/s during your project. An effective way to keep your supervisor in the loop on your work as you go along is to cc them into any emails relating to your research. It allows them to keep track of relevant conversations and gives you a bit of clout if you're asking for help or access to resources.

A common way of conducting a student–supervisor relationship that includes multiple supervisors is to have a main supervisor, who (as the role suggests) is your main point of contact and support throughout your research, and a second supervisor, who can offer advice on your topic, but who isn't as directly involved in the execution of the project.

The role of a researcher

When you are working on your project and writing up your dissertation, your role is as researcher. Even if you have been given a title to work on or a research question to answer, the work that you do and the research output is your responsibility. Take pride in the fact that your work will, by the very definition of research, add to the body of knowledge about your field – even if it adds only a tiny contribution. Because your research is 'yours', you should take responsibility for its direction and progression. Of course, you will be limited by time and equipment, but don't feel limited by anything else; if you want to change the focus of a pre-assigned question, for example, or add another element of investigation onto your allocated project, discuss this with your supervisor – they are unlikely to say no if your aims are realistic.

As a researcher, you are responsible for all of the practical and written work in your project. Although you may only be formally marked on your written output, you still may be expected to formulate a research question, and you are wholly responsible for the management of your desk-based and practical research. This means that if you need something, whether it be advice, equipment, time or space, you need to ask for it as it probably won't be offered to you as standard. Use your research project to build your confidence to ask for the tools and resources that you need. This will make you a better independent worker both in your degree and in your later career.

Avoiding and resolving differences

Thankfully, student–supervisor disputes are rare, but it helps to know how to resolve them and it is even better to know how to avoid them in the first place. The key to plain sailing in your student–supervisor relationship in clear boundaries, expectations and communication. It is a good idea to decide on acceptable forms of communication early on. Generally speaking, it's expected that you will both respond to emails in a timely manner, but that messages sent outside working hours will wait until either one of you is back 'in the office'. You will probably also decide a timescale for meetings (e.g. once a fortnight for an hour at a time). Find out, as well, their policy about knocking on their office door – some supervisors operate a more flexible open-door policy than others. Once you know how to get in touch, and how they will contact you, you'll feel more confident about reaching out to them when you need to.

In the first meeting with your supervisor, discuss the following:

1. How often will you meet?
2. Can you email them between meetings?
3. Will meetings be 1:1 or in a group?
4. Will they help you to source samples or equipment?
5. Will they give you feedback on your chapter plans or drafts?
6. Do you need to submit drafts to them on a regular basis?
7. Do you need to update them on your progress through the project?

In addition to defining how you'll communicate, it helps to find out how much support they are able to give you throughout your project. Levels of support vary greatly between subjects, degree level (undergraduate or postgraduate) and even individual supervisors. Don't assume that because your friend is meeting their supervisor weekly, that yours will do the same – it might be that your supervisor will offer more feedback on written work, or it might be that less hands-on supervision is more suited to your project. There may be a departmental policy that informs how and when you work with your supervisor. Managing their (and your) expectations of the project at the outset will avoid confusion stemming from miscommunication later down the line.

Being fully prepared for supervisor meetings will also help to avoid situations of conflict in the first place. A day or two in advance of every project meeting, check whether you have everything you'll need to enable an efficient and productive discussion. This means:

- sending any work you'd like them to read at least a week before the meeting if there is no formal deadline;
- writing down any questions or discussion points that you'd like to bring up;
- revisiting the last email conversation you had to make sure any small tasks you agreed have been completed.

Both your time and your supervisor's time is precious, and by being prepared, you stand the best chance of getting the most help and support possible out of each meeting you have. In addition to preparedness, proactively noting down tasks that both you and your supervisor agree to work on will show your intention to see these tasks through, as well as serve as a reminder for you after the meeting. Finally, after every meeting, a quick email to summarize the topics discussed and deadlines agreed will be helpful to you both in forming a record of your conversation.

Above all, the key to a successful student–supervisor relationship is the mutual respect of professional boundaries. Your supervisor should strive to follow through with any commitments they make regarding your project, give you any feedback they offer in a timely manner and to be available (via email at the least) if you require any help or support. In return, you should also aim to keep your supervisor up to date with your progress (again, via email) on a regular basis, complete work on time, and arrive at meetings prepared and engaged. If you treat the relationship as if your supervisor were your manager at work, you'll find the right perspective for your project.

Of course, it's also important to recognize that not every working relationship is smooth or successful all of the time. Thankfully, as mentioned earlier, clashes between supervisors and their students are rare.

Nevertheless, it's important to know how to deal with issues relating to your professional relationship, should they come up. Addressing any issues as soon as they arise will invariably be easier for all parties involved. Issues that remain unresolved may escalate and will become more difficult to untangle as time goes on. In addition, your project may only last a few weeks, so it makes sense to address any issues quickly so that you can use the time that you have in the most efficient way.

The way in which you approach potential issues and conflicts with your supervisor will influence the eventual outcome. An email is usually a good starting point for conflict resolution, especially if you feel strongly about the situation. Bringing any issues up in writing allows you to review and edit your statement, and even to save it and come back to it if needs be. A properly worded email will reduce miscommunication and provide a record of the matter at hand, should you need it. When bringing up issues, bear in mind that your supervisor might not even be aware that a problem exists. Speak to your supervisor about the problem, not their behaviour or your feelings about them: this avoids blaming language and ensures that the focus remains on solving the problem at hand so that you can get back on track with your project as soon as possible.

Dear Beth,

I received your email about rescheduling our latest scheduled meeting; I'm free on Tuesday afternoon or Thursday all day next week, if either of those days suit you?

I wondered if you might be able to provide some guidance on an issue I'm having with my data that I planned on bringing up in today's meeting? I have finished my data collection and have begun to analyse the results. I'm struggling, however, to identify the correct statistical test to use that best addresses my research question. This issue is preventing me from progressing any further with my report as I am unable to write about my results without the data processing. I'm also conscious that my deadline for submission is in three weeks' time, so I'd like to get the stats finished this week.

I've attached the raw data and my research question to this email, I'd be grateful if you could advise me via email or, if that isn't possible, if you could let me know who might be able to help me with this issue.

Best wishes,
Sam Hillway

In the example below, the student contacted their supervisor as they were frustrated with their lack of engagement. The supervisor had rearranged three project meetings at short notice, and the student had planned on using the meeting to ask for some guidance on the appropriate statistical tests to apply to their data. The project report deadline is in three weeks and the student feels unable to progress with their writing without this advice.

In the example above, the student has focused on their immediate problem, rather than the issue of their supervisor rearranging the meeting. That's not to say that the student isn't justified in feeling frustrated about their supervisor's actions, but voicing these frustrations doesn't necessarily overcome the hurdle relating to their data. Instead of focusing on a complaint, the student made a request for guidance and provided all of the information required (the data and the research question) to allow a quick response from their supervisor.

Resolving conflict – key points to remember

- Consider bringing any issues up in an email to start with, especially if you have strong feelings about the situation.
- Remember that your supervisor might not even be aware that there is a problem.
- Think about the language you use – focus on the problem, as opposed to your supervisor's actions or behaviour.
- Consider whether making a request, rather than voicing a complaint, will get things back on track more quickly.
- If you feel you cannot approach your supervisor, or if discussing the issue with your supervisor doesn't result in resolution, speak to the module leader or contact your student representative body and follow your university's policies on complaints.

The approach outlined above is suitable for resolving minor conflicts where a solution is possible and the relationship can continue after the issue is addressed. In situations where it isn't appropriate to engage with your supervisor, or you have attempted resolution without success, the next step is to follow your institution's complaints process. Quite often, your student representative body (such as the students' union) are able to provide support and signposting if you have a more significant issue with your supervisor that can't be solved between you. Your university will have policies and guidelines in place to effectively manage more serious problems and disputes, and it may be beneficial to be familiar with these so that you understand your rights as a student.

It's an unavoidable fact that dealing with professional disputes (whether large or small) can feel uncomfortable for all parties, but remember that it is your supervisor's job to support you and the obligation of your university to provide you with the tools and resources required to undertake your research. Maintain your professional conduct at all times and you'll very likely never need to consider the issue of conflict resolution. And even if you do, treat the situation as an opportunity to gather valuable experience – conflict resolution is a very common job interview topic, so at the very least, you'll have some experience to draw from!

How to make the most of your supervisor

Your supervisor is one of the most valuable resources you have access to during your research project. You should utilize their knowledge and expertise as much as possible throughout the practical and the written parts of your project – don't be afraid to ask! The list below illustrates some of the different ways in which your supervisor can help you through your project:

Planning

- **Providing specialist subject knowledge to help you shape your research question.** This might include advising on potential topics, or highlighting interesting papers that discuss gaps in the current literature.
- **Helping to procure working space, samples or equipment.** While the actual legwork will probably be your responsibility, your supervisor will know good sources of potential samples (e.g. archives or sites) and will be familiar with the processes involved in reserving any specialist equipment you might need.
- **Facilitating networking or introducing you to professional connections.** Networking is an invaluable career process that can be both daunting and difficult to get started as a student. You might want to speak to another academic or industry professional about opportunities, research interests, or even something as simple as borrowing equipment to collect data. In the first instance, speak to your supervisor to find out if they would be willing to introduce you to the person you're interested in speaking to.

Practical work

- **Advice on solving any issues that arise as you complete your data collection.** Your supervisor will very likely be familiar with the methods you are using to collect data for your research. They should be one of your first ports of call if you come across any problems with samples, equipment or data.
- **Help with interpreting raw data.** As your supervisor will probably be a subject specialist in your topic, they can also help with providing interpretations for tricky or inconclusive data. They won't do all of the work for you, and they will expect that you've had a decent go at interpreting the data before you approach them, but they may be happy to look over your data with you to confirm any theories that you develop from your data.

Writing

- **Guidance with searching the academic literature.** Again, you will be expected to direct the vast majority of the work relating to your desk-based research, but your supervisor can help identify appropriate databases and may point out some of the significant or relevant literature that is important to your work.
- **Giving feedback on writing quality.** It's unlikely that you'll get feedback on every aspect of your writing, but your supervisor may offer to look over a sample of your report to gauge the quality of your writing and provide some pointers on improving your drafts.

Post-dissertation

- **Providing job and further study application references.** Your supervisor may be one of the only staff members in you university that knows your abilities and working habits enough to provide a good-quality professional reference. If you have a good working relationship with your supervisor, they should be happy to act as your referee.
- **Getting your research published.** While this is less common for undergraduate students, if your research is of sufficient quality, your supervisor may support you in writing up your project as a journal article. They will provide advice on appropriate journals to target, as well as working with you to write the article itself. Make sure to credit your supervisor as co-author if you write an article together.
- **Acting as a mentor.** Your supervisor may be willing to offer you advice as you pursue your chosen career path after your degree. A brief email to ask their advice about a PhD programme that you're interested in, or a company that you're considering an application for is totally appropriate and staff are usually happy to share their expertise.

Other support structures you can use

While your supervisor is your first point of contact for anything relating to your research project, there are a huge variety of services and resources that exist in most universities to help students with their work. Take the time to find out what is offered in your individual institution, as the scope and delivery of these resources differs across the higher education sector.

Who can I go to?

The library	• Strategies for sourcing academic literature • Help with desk-based research skills • Referencing guides
Lab technicians	• Troubleshooting sample issues • Help with operating lab equipment • Advice on maintaining adequate health and safety
Academic development staff	• Help with critically evaluating the literature • Developing your academic writing skills • Advice on proofreading and editing your work
Peers/ PhD students	• Useful sources of support and lived experience • Good working habits • Moral support!
Subject academics	• Help with understanding subject-specialist concepts • Advice on using specialized equipment and/or databases • Advice about publishing and presenting at conferences
The IT department	• Access to referencing software • Training for specialist software packages (e.g. SPSS or MatLab) • Access to borrowed laptops and advice for purchasing your own equipment
Disability services	• Access to assistive technology • Arranging reasonable adjustments to courses and assessments • Help with referral for diagnosis of several physical and mental impairments
English for Academic Purposes	• Improving language skills for international students • Advice on written and spoken language as well as listening comprehension • Help with culture and intercultural awareness

Exercise 2: Considering supervisor styles

Take a look at Table 3 again and have a think about the following questions:

1. Which style of supervision do you think would suit you the most, and why?
2. Which style do you think would suit you the least, and why?
3. How would you make the most of the supervision styles you identified in the first two questions?

Next steps

	Research and approach your chosen academic if you are required to source your own supervisor
	Set up an initial supervisor meeting to discuss the project and your mutual expectations
	Prepare for the meeting by reading about your topic and making a note of topics you'd like to discuss
	Send an email to your supervisor following the first meeting to summarize what was discussed and tasks you'll complete before your next check-in with them

Planning your work

Introduction

Well-considered plans and good time management during your project will mean:

- You avoid unnecessary anxiety and feel more in control because you know where you are and what comes next.
- Emergencies and setbacks have less of an impact on your research because everything is completed in good time.
- Your work, both practical and written, is of high quality because you've thought about the order and structure in your plan.
- You enjoy your research, because you are productive, you can see tangible progress and you're able to take regular breaks.

If this is your first dissertation or project, though, the planning stage may seem a bit daunting because it's difficult to work out a timeline for something that you've never done before. Even if this is not your first research project, it is vital to take some time to think about a timetable and approach to the practical and desk-based parts of your work. This means that you will be able to complete your project in a timely manner and without a frantic rush at the end to write up (to the detriment of your final grade).

Topics in this chapter include:

- Time management and maintaining motivation
- Project planning
- Planning for potential challenges in your research.

Time management in research

Most academic researchers will tell you that they never have enough time for their work. From PhD student to professor, academics are constantly battling the passage of time. This is most likely because of many competing demands, but also because research is a long-term endeavour that takes weeks, months or even years to complete, and therefore requires careful planning to make sure that steady progress is made. A large project, such as a dissertation, can seem a daunting task to plan, especially if it is your first time conducting research. The key to a well-planned project is to manage your time from two perspectives: the big picture and the day-to-day work.

The big picture

Building the schedule for your research will take some time and thought, but it is an essential first step that many students skip, then later regret. Not only will each task in your research project take a different amount of time, but the time it will take you to collect your data for one project is not necessarily the same as the time it would take in a different project. In addition to these complexities, your research doesn't only have to fit in with your own schedule of work/study/general life but also with your supervisor's schedule and with your institution's resource schedule – this is where the thought comes in. It might take a week or two to finalize your plan, but you can make your plan while you are also working on the beginning stages of defining your project.

A step-by-step process for planning your research

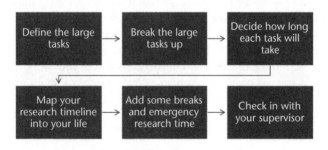

Step 1: Define the large tasks

The first step to planning a large project is defining the large, milestone tasks that you'll need to complete.

For a typical research project, this could include:

1. Picking your project.
2. Defining your research questions.
3. Conducting a desk-based literature review.
4. Conducting practical lab or field work.

5. Writing the chapters of your report or dissertation.
6. Proofreading and submission.

Step 2: Break the large tasks up

Once you have defined your big tasks, you can begin to split these up into sub-tasks. For example:

1. Picking your project
   - Choose a project from the options and submit a project intention form.
   - Contact supervisor to set up initial meeting.
   - Do some broad background reading on the topic.

2. Conducting a desk-based literature review
   - Define key topics related to your research questions.
   - Define keyword searches for all topics.
   - Conduct literature search and filter out irrelevant papers.
   - Critically evaluate chosen papers.
   - Summarize academic opinion on the chosen topics.

Step 3: Decide how long each task will take

By now you'll be looking at a (probably quite long!) list of tasks that need to be accomplished to complete your project. It's now time to assign a reasonable amount of time to complete each task. Work in days, as opposed to hours and minutes, to make your plan simple and flexible. Don't think about how long something *should* take, rather think about how long you think it *will* take. Also don't get too bogged down in making accurate time predictions at this point – later down the line you'll be checking in with your supervisor who may tell you that, in their experience, a desk-based review takes more or less time than you've planned. For now, take an educated guess at time limits for each task and, when you have an estimation for each sub-task, collate the times to give you total time limits for your big tasks. See the example below for a guide.

Conducting a desk-based literature review (16 days in total)

- Define key topics related to your research questions (1 day)
- Define keyword searches for all topics (1 day)
- Conduct literature search and filter out irrelevant papers (3 days)
- Critically evaluate chosen papers (10 days)
- Summarize academic opinion on the chosen topics (1 day)

After completing this step for all your defined large tasks, take a look at the total amount of time you have estimated your research will take. This is the first checking-in point that will begin to refine and tailor your plan so that it is both comprehensive and realistic. When reviewing your total

Figure 2   A sample Gantt chart for a research project

time estimation for your project, calculate the number of weeks between now and hand-in and multiply the weeks by five (representing a five-day working week). The result should be broadly similar (give or take a few days) to your total estimated project days. If it is wildly over or under, go back and reassess each task before moving on to the next step in the process.

Once you have completed this step, it can be helpful to visualize your time in a Gantt chart. Figure 2 was created using mural.co, which is a free digital whiteboard with lots of useful templates for project planning and brainstorming.

Step 4: Map your research timeline into your life

The next stage of planning involves fitting your research into your life. There will be any number of personal and professional commitments that you will already have planned, and this step involves fitting your research around these (not necessarily the other way around) and potentially changing and prioritizing plans in busy periods.

The easiest way to complete this step is with an electronic calendar such as Google Calendar, Apple Calendar or Microsoft Outlook. The aim is to build a plan for your time for the whole period of your research. When prioritizing your time, plan your time in the following order.

1. All of your unavoidable commitments

   These commitments commonly include paid part-time work and studying other courses. It's okay if you don't know your exact schedule, for example if you work variable shifts and you haven't been given your rota yet. Simply block out the number of hours or days you know you'll be working that week. So, if you normally work twelve hours a week, block out any two working days of the week and you can refine this later.

2. All of the things you'd like to do

   These might be upcoming nights out, holidays that haven't yet been booked, day trips, etc. – anything that is optional, not set in stone and not absolutely essential. It may seem strange to plan the fun stuff before your research, but leisure time is important and will keep you motivated to work on your project.

3. Your research tasks

   Finally, fill the gaps in your timetable with your research. Hopefully, your planned research task will slot nicely around your life and you will have an accurate a realistic plan for your time over the coming weeks/ months. Sometimes, though, the research doesn't quite fit, and this is where you may need to find a balance between what you'd like to do and what you need to do. If you find yourself stretched for time, consider what you can move or drop to fit your research in.

A note about practical tasks

When thinking about your lab work or field work, it's worth considering that the times that you'll be able to conduct these tasks might be dictated by the availability of samples, equipment or space. Keep your practical task plans quite flexible until you can confirm access to anything you might need from your institution.

Step 5: Add some breaks and emergency research time

If you're undertaking a large project like a dissertation, you'll probably need a break from your research at some point in the process. A long weekend is usually enough to recharge your batteries and renew your motivation for the rest of your work; try to build in a planned break somewhere near the middle of your project. It's also good practice to have at least one day of the week (ideally two) for rest. This is where you only do the fun stuff, and you don't think about your project or other commitments. Regular breaks may not always be possible, and there may be a few late nights and lost weekends as you get towards hand-in but consider the days off that you plan to be a vital part of completing your research. Burn-out is a very real risk when taking on a large project alongside other commitments, and your breaks are your guard against this.

As well as planning some well-earned rest, you might want to see where you might allocate some 'emergency' research time in your timetable. This is an extra cushion of flexibility that you build into your schedule that allows for parts of your project to take longer than planned without it negatively impacting your final submission. Good places to protect a day or so of emergency time is towards the end of your practical work, and during the writing of your literature review and discussion chapters. These tasks always seem to take longer than you plan and, if you can, it is useful to add up to 10-20 percent per cent of your planned time as emergency time.

Step 6: Check in with your supervisor

Now that you have a well-considered list of tasks mapped onto a timetable that you know works for you, you can take this to your supervisor for their advice and opinion. Either send them an electronic copy or take along a printed version of your plan. If you wanted to share the research plan only (and not your other personal and professional plans) consider making a Gantt chart for your supervisor to review (see Table 5 on recommended software). Questions that you should consider asking your supervisor at this point are:

1. In their experience, does your timeline seem feasible for the project you're doing?
2. Can your supervisor work with that timetable? They may be on a research trip at a crucial point in your plan, for example.
3. How do you access equipment/space for your practical work so that you can firm up these parts of your plan?
4. Do they think you've missed anything important?

Once your supervisor has seen your plan, spend some time making any adjustments you think are necessary.

Once you have your plan …

Your finished plan should be something that you use and refer to throughout your project. The most visible way of displaying your research schedule is on a wall planner. Simply mark up your tasks on a calendar and stick it on your wall near to where you work. A second option is to use a project management app that sends notifications when tasks are due or are late (see the recommended software in Table 5 for some suggestions). An alternative (but less in-your-face) method is saving your plan onto the desktop of your computer and make a habit of having it open in the background while you work. Whichever approach you choose, make sure that you don't spend your valuable time making a research plan that you never refer to. It should be an ever-present guide as you work through your project.

Day-to-day time management

Good study habits will help you to stick to your research plan. You might already be confident in keeping yourself motivated and organizing your time, but if your habits are less than ideal, it is better to make small adjustments to how you approach work rather than planning a radical turnaround of behaviour that is less likely to become habit. The four ideas below will help you to stay on track. If they are new to you, try them out one at a time and they will eventually become part of your natural working rhythm.

1. Set a goal

Your long-term research plan will provide you with deadlines along the way to help you keep track of your work. Goals that are a couple of weeks down the road are sometimes difficult to work on, however. Whenever you work on your project, set yourself a goal for that day. You might define your goal by tasks completed. For example, you might want to write a thousand words or weigh twelve samples. Task-based goals don't have a time limit, so you simply work on your tasks until they are done. If you would rather work for a defined amount of time, set yourself a time-based goal. For example, you will write for two hours or weigh out samples for half an hour. There's no need to always stick to one type of goal throughout your research. Change the type of goal based on how motivated you're feeling, what you need to get done, how much time you have or even just how you'd prefer to work. You might want to write down your goal, but quite often simply defining the goal in your head is enough to keep yourself motivated.

Why it works:

Defining a goal gives you something to work towards. You know when you have completed your work and you feel a sense of accomplishment when you achieve your goal. Working without a goal, on the other hand, is aimless. There is no definite measure of progress, and it's difficult to maintain motivation as a result.

2. Plan your time. Track your progress

This technique is a simple method of staying on task when you're working on ongoing research tasks such as writing and measuring large amounts of samples. Referring to your long-term plan, identify the deadline for completing your task. Divide the total hours that you've assigned for that task into the number of weeks or days you have to complete it. This gives you a realistic set amount of hours to work on the task per day/week. Map those hours out into a simple Excel table, and tick them off as you progress through the week. In practice, there will be times when you go over or under your planned working hours, but mapping large tasks this way will help you to visualize your progress and to recognize if you are falling behind.

For example, if you are required to write approximately ten thousand words for your dissertation and you have six weeks to complete the writing, 10,000/6 = 1,667. You must write 1,667 words per week to complete your writing. This can then be broken down in to working days. For example, if you have planned to work for four days per week on your research, 1,667/4 = 416. You must write 416 words per day to reach your goal. Round this value up to the nearest 50, and create a table.

The example below shows the ten-thousand-word dissertation mapped out over six weeks, with four working days per week. We can see the darker grey boxes that show where the target was met or exceeded, and strikethroughs are used to show where the weekly goal was missed. Using this simple method, you can get a good idea of where you are with your writing progress at a glance.

Why it works:

Mapping out larger tasks in this way is essentially a Gantt chart for individual tasks. Breaking down the task into manageable chunks makes the whole undertaking feel a lot less daunting and a lot more realistic. As the famous saying goes, how do you eat an elephant? One bite at a time.

	Daily word count achieved			
Week 1	457/450	~~436/450~~	456/450	560/450
Week 2	470/450	492/450	~~395/450~~	~~256/450~~
Week 3	463/450	~~397/450~~	/450	/450
Week 4	/450	/450	/450	/450
Week 5	/450	/450	/450	/450
Week 6	/450	/450	/450	/450

Table 4   A ten-thousand-word dissertation planned over six weeks

3. Work on one of three things

Quite often in academic research, there are multiple tasks that require your attention in the same week. You may be reading for your literature review as you complete your practical work, and also writing your methods chapter. On top of these central research tasks, there are all the little things that go along with a substantial project: emails to supervisors, trips to the library, looking up formatting rules for your institution, etc. With potentially several different things that you could be working on when you sit down to work, it can sometimes be difficult to decide what to do and to keep on task. It's very easy to get distracted from writing by the spontaneous decision to prepare for a meeting later in the week.

The following approach works nicely in conjunction with a time-planning goal (described above). To prevent distraction and procrastination, decide on three jobs that you will work on during your study session. Make at least one of your jobs a substantial, ongoing task that you're working on at the moment, but one or two of your tasks could be smaller, quicker jobs that you would normally get distracted by. Write your three tasks down on a sticky note and stick it on your desk or computer monitor (somewhere that is visible while you work). For the whole of that working session, you are allowed to work on any one of those three tasks. You don't have to do them in order, and you can swap between the tasks at any time. If you glance at your sticky note and realize that what you're working on isn't on your list, that's a good indicator that you're procrastinating. Half of the battle with procrastination is knowing that you're doing it in the first place, so this technique is a particularly good one if you sit down with the intention of writing a chapter of your dissertation but find yourself an hour later writing an email to your supervisor. Be sure to tick off each task when it is complete.

Why it works:

Defining three tasks to work on gives you a flexible but focused list of activities that you have decided are productive. You can choose to move on to any of the tasks at any time during your working session, allowing a safe way of being distracted from larger (more boring!) tasks. Visually ticking off the tasks as you complete them also shows tangible progress and fosters motivation to complete those larger tasks one you've finished the little ones.

4. Read/write in short bursts with small breaks

There are some research tasks that require your focus for long periods of time: reading journal articles and writing your report are two typical examples. Maintaining focus over a few hours can be difficult, and as a result, progress can be slow. Steady, tangible progress is the key to fostering and maintaining motivation.

When you're sitting down to work on a task for more than an hour, think about breaking up and completing the task in short bursts with small (around five-minute) breaks. This approach is known as the pomodoro time-management technique. The efficacy of the pomodoro technique can be increased with the use of a timer or a dedicated app (see the recommended software in Table 5). To use the approach, decide on a goal for the full time that you're working on a particular task that day. You might, for example, be writing the discussion chapter of your report for four hours, and you'd like to write two thousand words that day.

If you're aiming to write two thousand words over four hours, it makes sense to aim for five hundred words per hour. Set a timer for 50 minutes and aim to only work on writing during that period. Don't check your emails, don't look at data, don't read the literature – just write! An app such as Forest can help you avoid the distraction of your phone by displaying a timer that grows a tree and disables access to certain apps as you work. When the timer is up, check in on your progress. Did you write your five hundred words? Were you distracted, or did you stay focused for the whole 50 minutes? Report your progress back if you're working in a group and take a ten-minute break to stretch your legs, chat about writing tips or have a rant about your samples producing random values. When your ten minutes is up, set off a new timer and start writing. If you plan on working for more than three or four hours, plan a longer break in the middle of your day to get away from your desk.

Why it works:

Working in short 45–50 minute bursts means that you are always working towards an easily attainable goal. Your mind gets a rest in between each burst, so that you feel refreshed for the next session. The break also gives you a chance to take stock of your progress, which then motivates you for the next part of your work.

Recommended software

This list is not exhaustive, but does suggest some helpful apps and software.

Software	Description	Found at	Cost	Mobile friendly?
Forest	This flexible timer has an additional in-built procrastination booster. Starting a timer plants a tree which dies if you leave the app. You earn coins for every tree successfully grown which you can use to plant real trees.	https://www.forestapp.cc/ App store/Google Play	About the price of a coffee.	Very.
TomatoTimer	A simple, no-nonsense timer that can time a pomodoro (a working session), a short break and a long break.	tomato-timer.com/	Free.	The website is mobile friendly.
Microsoft Excel	A spreadsheet programme that can be used to build Gantt charts and timetables.	Part of the Microsoft Office package.	Part of the Microsoft Office package. Free, if your institution uses Office 365.	Not really.
Clickup	A comprehensive and customizable project management tool used to set goals, plan your time and check off your tasks.	Clickup.com App store/Google Play	Free for the basic package (which is adequate for a single user).	Very.
Monday.com	Slick project management tool that can be used to plan a project and track individual tasks.	Monday.com App store/Google Play	Free for the individual package (adequate for a single user).	Very.

Table 5 Recommendations for time-management software

5. Work with a writing buddy

One of the most effective ways to maintain productivity and motivation when you are writing a substantial report or dissertation is to enlist the help of a writing buddy. A writing buddy can be anyone who is willing to work with you – a fellow student or not – but they will need to have something that they are working on too for it to be mutually beneficial. It also helps if what they are working on will take a similar amount of time for you to write your report, so a friend who is also writing their dissertation is ideal.

Meeting online is usually more productive than meeting in person because it stops too much socializing, and platforms such as Discord or Zoom are ideal for writing buddy sessions. Plan three or four two-hour sessions a week and work using the pomodoro technique detailed above. You might want to share writing and productivity tips between you, but be careful not to comment directly on each other's work to avoid accidental plagiarism.

Why it works:

Working with a buddy holds you accountable. You are more likely to start working at your planned time and maintain productivity when you are working if you know that someone else is working with you. The satisfaction of finishing sections and chapters of your work is also greater because you can share your successes with each other. I can personally attest to the effectiveness of this method because it is how I wrote this book! Seriously, this book would not exist if it wasn't for my colleague, Elina.

Overcoming obstacles and challenges

Setbacks and obstacles are a normal and expected feature of scientific research. The very nature of research means that you're dealing with some unknowns, so it's inevitable that sometimes things don't go to plan. Factor in human error and some unreliable equipment, and there's bound to be a hiccup at some point in your project. Setbacks in research can usually be attributed to one of two things: factors beyond your control (e.g. a fellow student accidentally defrosts your temperature sensitive samples), or poor planning (e.g. you plan to collect seaweed from the tideline, but you get to the location at high-tide). You can't influence the first, so getting your planning right will prevent or minimize the effect of setbacks that you can influence. Your success in overcoming all challenges is defined by your reaction to them. Some setbacks can seem insurmountable, but with a strategy and some support, it's surprising what you can overcome.

The problem-solving plan

You will probably not be able to anticipate the challenges you might face as you progress through your research. That is absolutely fine. What you can do to prepare for any setbacks is to have a formula for solving any problems you come across. Having a step-by-step plan for problem solving means that you feel more prepared to tackle any issues, and you're more likely to solve them more quickly than if you didn't have a prepared plan.

Step 1. Identify your problem

You might be aware that there is a problem, but you're maybe not so sure what the source of that problem is. This happens more than you'd expect in research, so the crucial first step to solving any problem is to define it. For example, your lab work might not be going well. Everything is taking far longer than you had planned and you're running out of your booked time in the lab. To begin solving this, you have to get down to specifics. The root of this problem could lie in several different places: maybe your initial plan was too ambitious, or perhaps there's a problem with your method. Narrowing down the source of the problem is an important first step and the key to finding a solution.

Step 2. Break your solution down into small tasks

Once you have identified your specific problem, you can start to build a way out of it. The solution to a problem is rarely straightforward, however, and it may be easier to navigate if you break down your solution into small tasks. For example, if you find that the problem is connected to your method, you'll need to identify which step or steps of the method are problematic. Your tasks might be:

- Read the method you're using step by step to check for misinterpretations.
- Check all equipment is in good working order.
- Check all reagents are in date and diluted to the correct strength.
- Prepare one or two samples and observe the reaction at every step.

Define your tasks and work through them one by one until you have either solved the problem or reached the end of your list without finding a solution. This step is particularly important because it gives you a finite list to work on, therefore preventing the issue of getting stuck on a problem or going in circles to find a solution.

Step 3. Identify any support or resources that you need

You may be able to solve many of the challenges you come across during your research without any additional help. Inevitably, though, there will be some instances where you need extra resources (e.g books or equipment) or extra support (e.g. advice from a lab tech). Once you have completed step 2, think about anything that you might need to help you implement a solution. For example, you might discover that one of the chemicals you use for your prep is out of date, so you need the lab technician to order some more. Alternatively, you might finish working through your tasks and be no closer to a solution, in which case it's probably time to speak to your supervisor. See Chapter 2 for ideas of other sources of support that you might seek out.

Step 4. Check in with your research plan

Once you have addressed your problem, don't move on without revisiting your research plan. Go back and have a look at your Gantt chart (or equivalent) and check that you can still accomplish everything you planned to in the time you have left. An unfortunate side-effect of research challenges is that they often have a knock-on effect to the rest of your plan, but you can avoid this by reviewing and updating your timeline as you go.

Common academic challenges

Unexpected data

Many research students begin to panic if their results don't conform to their expectations. Perhaps they don't prove your central hypothesis. They could be entirely random and you're unable to answer your research question. Most commonly, you'll have one or two datapoints that are outliers and you're not sure why they don't conform to the trend that the rest of your results follow. The thing to remember with unexpected results is that they are not a barrier to a good grade. You are marked on the quality of your written report and if you can explain your results, you are demonstrating good-quality research.

The following key points show you how to deal with wonky data.

1. Don't hide it! The worst thing you can do it either not report the result or to report a different, fabricated result in its place. This is unethical research practice. You must report and acknowledge every result you obtain in your research.
2. Report data outside quality control indicators (QCIs). Some subjects, such as analytical chemistry, require the application of quality control indicators to results. These tests ensure that only good-quality data is discussed when answering research questions. If you have poor-quality

data, don't just discard it. Report it in your results chapter, highlight the datapoints that don't meet QCIs and state that you won't be discussing the data. You can only discard data from discussion if you have a valid reason for doing so.

3. Explain the reason/s for unexpected data. The key to dealing with wayward data is to offer a reasonable explanation for the results. If you're struggling to explain certain datapoints, look back at your lab notes for clues. Could the sample be contaminated? Could there have been a mistake in one of the pre-treatment steps? Could the sample be an outlier because of some natural variation in the population? Report in the discussion chapter the reasons for the unexpected results and, if the reason is human error, offer a method of avoiding the same error in future research. Ultimately, you may not be able to pin down a single reason for outlying data, and in this case you should outline the potential causes and then weigh up the likelihood of each being true.

If you're struggling with data interpretation, speak to your supervisor. They will be able to help you navigate your results. The one take-home point to remember about unexpected data is to explain it, don't hide it.

Procrastination

Procrastination is the bane of all academic researchers. It is also a normal part of academia that you will never be able to fully prevent. Some procrastination can be useful – you might come up with a new way of interpreting your data while you tidy your room instead of writing your report. I, personally, had so many PhD-related epiphanies while washing the pots that I would find myself in the kitchen at 1:00 am in a bid to stimulate ideas. The point at which procrastination becomes problematic is when it begins significantly hindering progress and causing stress. This is when it needs addressing.

If your procrastination comes from a lack of motivation, a different approach is required. Self-motivation can be difficult to muster, especially when you're working on a long project with a deadline that is weeks away. The problem with a lack of motivation is that it induces anxiety as you worry about not working. Anxiety is never conducive to self-motivation and progress, so you delay work even more. The anxiety-motivation cycle can be a vicious one and the way to break it is to change your mindset about what fosters motivation. Many researchers wait until they feel ready to begin a task, but inevitably they never feel ready to start a task that they are putting off, and so they never get started. Instead of waiting until motivation to work hits you, turn on your computer or pull on your lab coat and do some work on the task for five minutes. Five minutes isn't daunting. You could easily spend more than that amount of time worrying about the work! The magic of spending a few minutes on a task you've been putting off is that it will spark your motivation. You will probably find that you've built up the task in your mind and, actually, it's a lot easier than you thought it was going to be. When you've finished your five minutes, you will also probably see the thing that you've been looking for while you've been procrastinating: progress! Progress stimulates more progress and, before you know it, you'll be in your research groove and back on track to complete your project.

Coping with personal challenges

As well as your research, you will have your personal life to manage. Keeping a good work/life balance is important, but sometimes life presents its own challenges that you should address. Personal challenges can range from having a mild cold that makes you feel tired and unmotivated for a couple of days, right up to the most serious of personal issues such as relationship breakdown and bereavement. You can't (and shouldn't!) plan for every eventuality but keeping some resilience strategies in mind can help you mitigate the effect of personal challenges on your research.

Take a step back

Let's address the serious stuff first. Life events that cause long-term or severe short-term stress should be dealt with as a priority. Sometimes the best course of action is to step away from your research for a while until you have dealt with your current challenges. This is particularly true when experiencing trauma or mental health issues. Speak to your supervisor about a suspension or extension – every institution has procedures in place that allow students with mitigating circumstances to take a break from their studies so that serious personal issues do not affect their education. The worst thing you can do when you are going through a tough time is to ignore it and try to get on with your research regardless. You'll only end up doing a terrible job of your work and chances are that your personal challenges won't diminish either. Far better to take a step back from your project, focus on your life and then get back to work when you're more able.

Actively manage stress

Stress (whether work-related or not) should be actively managed as a part of your day-to-day life. Students who regularly practise well-being strategies are more resilient and more successful in their studies. Actively managing your well-being includes:

- Recognizing when you're stressed. Indicators could be, for example broken sleep, irritability, changing eating habits or a lack of focus, but everyone is different. What are your stress indicators?
- Take a short break. You have already built some breaks into your project timeline, but also take shorter impromptu breaks when you need it. This could be anything from a day off that you had originally planned to use for writing, or a half hour break away from your desk. When stress is prohibiting progress, a break can do wonders.
- Plan things that you enjoy (and make some of these things healthy!). Taking part in something you enjoy will always positively affect your well-being. Socialize with friends, bake, go shopping – whatever you like to do. You'll find yourself refreshed and ready to work once you're finished.
- Try to keep work and life separate. This is easier said than done, but consciously avoid thinking about work while you are trying to relax. You can make this easier by having a dedicated workspace, if possible. If this isn't realistic, be sure to pack away your books and papers, and to turn your computer off if you're not using it.

Prioritize your health

As well as actively managing stress when it arises, there are things you can do to prevent personal challenges negatively affecting your research. Looking after your physical and mental health is always a good idea, but it is particularly important when you're under periods of increased stress. Schedule in some weekly exercise that you enjoy, and keep your fitness goals modest – now is not the time to aim for that marathon if you've never been running before. Physical exercise is also good for your mental health, but think about trying meditation or mindfulness as well. Yoga is one of the best exercises you can do as it encompasses both physical and mental well-being. Whatever you decide to do, make it a regular part of your timetable throughout your research.

Know your support structures

Just like problem solving an academic challenge, personal challenges often require access to external resources. Your first port of call for support is your supervisor. While they probably won't be the one to help you solve your issues, they will be able to signpost you to appropriate support and let you know your options for delaying or extending your studies. One of the support services your supervisor will most likely point you towards is your institution's counselling and well-being service. Most universities have extensive student mental health support that is free to access. Information about these services is usually readily available on their websites. The other valuable service to keep in mind is your GP – remember to register with your local doctor if you are living away from home at university. There are many different treatment options for mental health issues that your GP can help you with, ranging from medication to talking therapy. You may never need these sorts of support structures, but it always better to be aware of them and never use them than to need them and not know they are there.

Conclusion

This chapter asks you to think about a lot, from how you will use your time, to contingency planning in preparation for things not going to plan. If you consider all of these points, though, you will find your work easier to navigate, you'll feel less time pressure, and you'll be more resilient in the face of challenges. The essence of project management is breaking down large tasks into manageable chunks. It applies to so many different circumstances that you'll come across during your research, whether you're planning your entire project, sitting down at your desk to work for a couple of hours or problem solving a current challenge. Finally, keep in mind that challenges do happen, but every one is manageable and surmountable and, most importantly, you are surrounded by an institution and a lot of people who want you to succeed.

Next steps

	Take some time to work through the process for planning your research discussed at the beginning of this chapter
	Think about how you will manage your day-to-day workload
	Go to your institutions' website and look for all the different support services that are available to you as a research student. Bookmark the pages that you think may be useful

Collecting your data

Introduction

This chapter discusses the important subject of maintaining good practice during the data collection stage of your research. Taking the time to consider good data collection procedures will not only make your research easier because you will have all of the information you need to write a high-quality report, it will make it credible as well.

Topics in this chapter include:

- The value of good practice in scientific research
- Using the scientific method to demonstrate good practice
- Some good practice considerations during data collection.

Why is good practice important?

Research integrity and good academic practice is the absolute cornerstone of science and academia. Luckily, even if this is your first research project, you will have already learned many of these important principles as part of your degree course. The problem is that good practice is often taught implicitly, meaning that you probably won't have had specific classes or assessments on the subject, but good practice will have formed an integral part of your practical and theoretical education. So, it is important that you make yourself aware of what good practice means in your subject and what that might mean for your dissertation.

Good practice in science means that researchers are always honest and transparent in their work. You are now one of those researchers! Science relies on the honesty of experts to report what worked and what didn't work so that future studies can build on this knowledge. If just one scientist exaggerates their findings or lies about an experiment that failed, any subsequent research will be based on a fabrication and could therefore be discredited. This would cost institutions heavily in both time and money and, more importantly, scientific advances would be hindered. So, honesty and transparency in your dissertation is imperative to your success.

How do I maintain good practice throughout my dissertation?

Good-quality scientific research can be achieved by following the scientific method. This method, used in all science subjects, ensures that valuable questions are asked, reasonable hypotheses are developed and the method of testing these hypotheses are credible and robust. By following this method (illustrated in Figure 3) during your research project, you are emulating the same approach that professional scientists use when working on their own projects. There are some key considerations that you must take into account when working through the scientific method – these are discussed below.

Develop informed research questions and a balanced hypothesis

Good research is driven by carefully considered research questions. You will begin your dissertation journey in one of two ways: you will be required to propose a topic for your research yourself, or you may be given a topic by your department or your supervisor. Either way, you should think about the specific research questions that your dissertation will ask – all of your work will contribute towards answering those questions.

Figure 3   A diagram of the scientific method

Take some time to consider and define your research questions. Developing your research questions may involve discussion with your supervisor and will invariably include reading up on the latest research developments in your topic. When thinking about your research questions, you should consider what is already known about your topic, what is not known and what the problem is that you are specifically trying to solve in your work. Your initial questions may change slightly as you read through the literature and gain a deeper knowledge of your subject, but, broadly speaking, your dissertation will be far easier if you break your topic down into three to five realistic questions at the start of your project.

Research questions work better when they are clear, specific and achievable. Remember that the purpose of your dissertation is to produce an original piece of research in your field. Your research questions should break down your research topic into bite-sized chunks and should avoid the typical pitfalls that poorly considered questions suffer from. See Table 6 for a comparison of good and poor-quality research questions.

Once you have informed research questions, you can begin to develop your hypothesis. This is a prediction of what you expect to see in your

	Good quality	Poor quality
Detailed	What is the current understanding of the environmental and economic factors of wind power in the academic literature?	What are the advantages and disadvantages of wind power?
Informed	Are there detectable differences in the $\delta^{13}C$ and $\delta^{15}N$ measurements of bone collagen samples that have been pre-treated using a method that includes an NaOH step (DeNiro and Epstein 1981) vs. a method that uses Ultrafilters (Brown et al. 1988).	What is the best pre-treatment method for the extraction of bone collagen for isotope ratio mass spectrometry?
Clear	Do regular one-to-one interactions with trained pet therapy dogs increase the quality of life of elderly residents living in UK care homes?	Do dogs benefit the elderly when they visit them?
Realistic	How can we make proton-beam therapy treatment for brain tumours more economically accessible in the UK?	What is the cure for cancer?

Table 6   Understanding the difference between good-quality and poor-quality research questions

results based on what is already known about the topic. You may choose to define your null and alternative hypothesis: the null hypothesis being the expected outcome and the alternative hypothesis being the opposite. Defining your research questions and hypotheses at the beginning of your research makes the discussion of your data in the report much easier as you can directly address these to show the outcome of your work.

Test your hypothesis using reliable and robust methods

When choosing the appropriate method for your research, think about what information you will need to answer your research questions. Common methodological approaches in science dissertations include:

- Designing an experiment under controlled conditions.
- Collecting and analysing secondary data, either from an archive or from published literature (a literature review).
- Making observations in the field across a defined time and space.
- Designing and testing a product. This could be something physical, like a traffic sensor, or something non-physical, like a computer programme.
- Collecting and analysing survey, interview and/or focus group data.
- A mixture of the approaches above, often called a multi-methodological approach.

You may have questions about which approach is most appropriate to answering your research questions, and your supervisor will be able to help you to find the right one. Whatever method you choose to apply in your project, make sure that you describe it clearly and concisely in a materials and methods chapter (see Chapter 8 for more guidance on writing this chapter). It is essential that, once you have chosen your method, you stick to it consistently during the practical part of your dissertation; don't add in or miss out steps, otherwise your data will be incomparable and therefore useless. You may need to undertake a small pilot study to test your method if it is either newly developed or has been adapted for your project. It is far better to test your method with a handful of practice samples before diving into your practical work as this means that you can make any necessary adjustments to the approach before you start the real work. Speak to your supervisor if you think a pilot study is appropriate for your dissertation.

Don't forget about ethical implications

Scientific research often comes with ethical implications. These formal processes ensure that good practice is upheld and that scientists are held accountable for their research. For dissertations, ethical implications will vary according to subject, but may include legal notices such as GDPR (General Data Protection Regulations), COSHH (control of substances hazardous to health) forms, ethical approval board applications or other formal processes. Your supervisor will be able to advise you on the specifics for your subject and your individual project, but it is important that you've considered potential ethical issues relating to your dissertation (and you might pick up some Brownie points by asking about ethical approval early on in your meetings!). Ethical issues in your field are not something to be rushed through at the beginning of your dissertation. If you intend to work in your degree field, you could end up dealing with these issues on a daily basis. Making yourself aware of ethics at this point will mean that you'll be able to impress potential employers with your professional and conscientious approach to this important subject.

So, what kinds of ethical issues might you need to consider?

- If you are dealing with human subjects, their human rights need to be considered.
- If you are collecting personal data, the privacy of your participants is important.
- If you are handling human bodies, organs or tissues that are under a hundred years old, there are strict regulations that need to be followed.
- If you are handling sensitive material or information, you will have to consider issues of confidentiality.
- If you are undertaking any dangerous work, there will be safety considerations to make (more on this below).
- If your research may cause reputational harm to an individual or an organization, the validity of this needs to be considered.

Conduct a thorough risk assessment

Science sometimes comes with some inherent dangers and it is important that all potential hazards are safely managed through proper risk assessment. COSHH are a mandatory element of risk assessment that must be carried out before you begin any practical work that involves hazardous chemical or biological agents. Your department may have their own pre-filled form or you may have to undertake your own risk assessment. You should speak to your supervisor about risk assessment before you undertake any practical work to ensure that you have completed any necessary paperwork and training so that you can safely use any specialist scientific equipment.

How do I maintain good practice in my practical work?

If you are to report your findings in an honest and transparent way in your dissertation, you *must* keep full and accurate lab or field notes while you are collecting data. You don't want to get to the writing stage of your dissertation and discover that you have gaps in your notes. There is nothing you can do to replace missing information, so make sure you note everything that might be relevant during your practical work.

As a science student, you will probably be used to keeping a lab book or field notebook. Not much will differ in the way you collect data for your dissertation, but be aware that you won't have your lab partner to fall back on for notes and that your dissertation is worth a large percentage of your total degree mark. Your dissertation is also likely to be the largest research project you've undertaken in your degree so far – it will very probably involve more data collected over a longer period of time, so you need to be organized. If you are a bit shaky with your record keeping, now is the time to brush up those skills!

Here are some key features of good-quality lab/field notes (see Figure 4 for an annotated example of well-organized notes):

- They are kept in one notebook with no loose papers tucked in the pages.
- Each new day of data collection begins on a new page with the date and a brief (one-line) entry about the data you are collecting and the method you are using.
- Hand-drawn tables are properly labelled with table headers.
- Units of measurement (°C, %, cm, g, etc.) are always used after values.
- Any anomalies observed in samples/protocol/sampling environment are clearly described.
- Essential data is digitally backed up, perhaps in a spreadsheet saved in multiple places.

You should also consider how you take notes as you progress through each part of your practical work. You will need to be quick in your note-taking, so think about what information you need to record and what you might need to know when you have your results. Do you need to set up a template in advance so that you can quickly and accurately take notes? For example, if you are measuring lots of samples at a balance, it makes sense to draw out a table with columns for the sample ID, the weight and any other variable you need to record. It is easy then to just work your way down the table to produce something that is neat and will make sense much later down the line. Taking a moment to consider how you will approach your note-taking before you start will become second nature as you progress through your practical work.

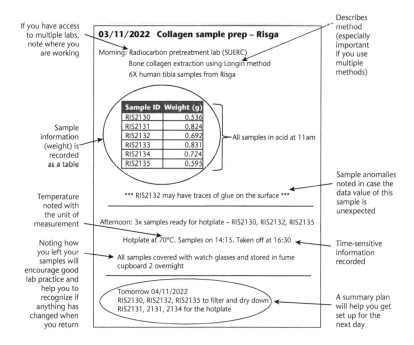

Figure 4 An example of some lab notes taken for a chemistry pre-treatment protocol

Above all, if something goes wrong – if you contaminate a sample or select the wrong programme settings, if you use the incorrect equipment or miss a data collection interval – don't worry! Record the error and move on. Mistakes happen in the field and in the lab because (believe it or not) scientists are human! The worst thing you could do is manipulate your notes or omit an entry in your lab book to hide your mistake. Your research instantly becomes discredited and it will be all for nothing because, after all, it is still perfectly possible to get a top grade in your dissertation with flawed data (see Chapter 7 to find out more about discussing wonky data).

Be honest and realistic in your interpretation of results

Once you have finished your data collection, it's time to interpret your results. It goes without saying that you should never fabricate, omit or amend your results to serve your own best interests. All of your data should be fully and honestly reported. It is not just your results that should be honest, but your *interpretation* of what the results mean in relation to your research questions should be as well. This means that you should strive to be as objective as possible when analysing your data to either confirm or refute your main hypothesis. Don't exaggerate your findings, leave out statistical tests that you know will not benefit your initial predictions or ignore anomalous data.

At the end of the day, science is often a muddy and blurred discipline. Where you have evidence to support an argument, you should absolutely state your findings with confidence. If, however, as is often the case, your results are not so clear-cut, make sure that you exercise caution in your interpretation (see Chapter 7 for more about how to talk about data in your writing). It is far better to be honest and say that your results don't definitively answer your research question and to suggest possible future directions in research than to over-confidently state that you have answered your question using weak evidence. A negative (or even an uncertain) result is still a useful result because we are then able to rule out certain approaches to investigating that particular question.

Next steps

	Take some time to plan how you will collect and store your data
	Make a list of materials you will need to maintain good record keeping
	Think about the ethical implications of your project. Make a list of potential issues and discuss these with your supervisor

6

Finding and analysing the literature

Introduction

A large part of academic research, whether a short project or a substantial dissertation, involves reading and discussing the published literature on your topic.

Topics in this chapter include:

- Using academic databases
- Deciding on the papers to read
- Conducting a balanced critical analysis of the literature
- Making notes and organizing your papers.

Why do I need evidence from the literature?

Discussing the academic literature in your research proves the breadth and depth of your knowledge about a subject. The way you incorporate and use evidence from the literature in your research report will be evaluated by your marker, and taken into account when deciding your grade. In addition, any academic research that relies solely on the data produced by the authors is essentially useless without the context that external evidence gives. There are a variety of reasons for finding and incorporating evidence from the literature:

- You will need to show what is already known about your topic to demonstrate your understanding of the area of research and to show where your work fits within the literature.
- Showing the gaps in the collective academic knowledge or the problems that are discussed within the literature will provide justification for your research.
- Comparing your results to the literature demonstrates your contribution to the knowledge.
- Information from the literature can be used to strengthen your claims about your findings and their implications.

What doesn't need evidence?	What needs accompanying evidence?
Any statement that 'belongs' to you or doesn't 'belong' to anyone (an individual or an institution):	Any statement that you can attribute to someone else (an individual or an institution):
• Common knowledge in your subject. • Facts that are widely accepted and not controversial. • Standard unpublished methods and protocols. • Your own methods, data, ideas, theories, images or conclusions. • The summary or conclusion of previously discussed ideas.	• A summary or description of published methods, data, ideas, theories images or conclusions. • Direct quotes. • A professional opinion (published or not).

Table 7 Statements in science writing that do and do not need accompanying external evidence

Sources of evidence

There is a huge variety of scientific evidence that you can (and should) incorporate into your writing. The best students use evidence from different types of sources, instead of relying on journal articles alone. Below is a list of possible sources you could consider exploring for your dissertation.

Academic journal articles are, by far, the most widely used sources of evidence in academic research. This is because the information in a journal article has been written by an expert in their field, scrutinized and approved by several other independent subject experts, and distributed in a publication that academics widely accept as being trustworthy and ethical. You can think of the contents of an academic journal as being a record of academic conversation; that is, the way in which new hypotheses and discoveries in your subject are revealed and debated.

Edited volumes are collections of work by different authors that are curated by an editor. Edited volumes are usually published as a printed book, and (like journal articles) are usually peer-reviewed by experts. Unlike journal articles, edited volumes usually discuss a broad topic within a subject, rather than being a single piece of research.

Monographs are usually printed books written by an author on a specialized subject. They are longer and more detailed than journal articles, but are peer-reviewed in much the same way.

Secondary data is raw data that was generated by somebody and then stored, usually, on institutional databases or in archives. This type of evidence is useful if you are unable to collect the type or volume of data you need for your research. Check before you use the data that it has not been published anywhere else (you will need to reference the publication if it has), and make sure that you are aware of the method of data collection so that you can be sure that the data is credible.

Grey literature is useful information that hasn't been published by a commercial or academic publisher. Grey literature includes documents such as conference proceedings, dissertations and lab procedures. Bear in mind that while you can verify the authors of grey literature, these types of evidence haven't always been subjected to the same rigorous review processes that published articles and books have.

Websites can be useful sources of secondary data, but be very careful about confirming the authenticity and authorship of any information you take from a website. Also bear in mind that webpages are much more fluid than books and articles, and can be edited frequently and, potentially, by someone who is not the original author.

Journalistic media (print or online) has its place in scientific research, but not as the communicator of scientific theories, ideas or facts (get those from the original source). Media sources are good for demonstrating what information is in the public sphere, what people care about and what public opinion is on a topic. Remember that media bias exists in every journalistic publication; make your reader aware of these biases when you use this type of evidence.

When do I read?

Don't let the first time you do a literature search be after you have finished the practical part of your project, just before you start writing. In fact, it is useful to begin reading from the very outset of your research project – before you even step foot in the lab or field. You will probably need to start exploring the literature while you are forming your research questions to give yourself some background knowledge and context (see Chapter 5 for advice on how to design research questions).

Once you begin reading, don't stop! Of course, you will need to spend time producing data and writing your dissertation, but get into the habit of relying on peer-reviewed journal articles to answer questions that arise as you progress through your project, rather than turning to textbooks or lecture notes (see the section below on reading to fill gaps in your knowledge for tips on getting started with this). This practice will give you a thorough and sophisticated understanding of your topic, and will result in a better-quality dissertation. Keeping up to date with ongoing work in your field will mean you won't miss any important publications that are relevant to your research. You may be working on your project over the course of several months, and science can move quickly in that time. Once you think you have exhausted the literature for your dissertation (usually once you have written your literature review), check in with the prominent journals in your subject on a regular basis. You may find new work that would make a useful inclusion to your dissertation and that a marker may expect to see discussed in the context of your topic.

Reading with a purpose

There are many different reasons for searching for and reading evidence during your project. Think about why you need to read the literature before you go looking for it – this will inform not only the topics you search for but also the types of literature you explore. Broadly speaking, there are three reasons why you might want to read the scientific literature: first, to fill gaps in your knowledge about your research area. This is a type of ongoing reading that you'll do throughout your project and your writing, and it is focused and the least in-depth type of reading. Secondly, reading to introduce and begin to address your research questions. This is the primary purpose of the literature review, so your reading for this should be comprehensive and exhaustive. Finally, reading to find evidence to support data analysis. This type of reading is carried out while you are analysing your results, ready to present in your discussion chapter. It is important to place your data within the context of the literature to add weight and credibility to your research.

Below is a guide to searching for literature in these three different circumstances.

Filling gaps in your knowledge

By searching the academic literature for answers to questions that crop up during the course of your research, instead of just relying on standard textbooks, you'll find that your gain a deeper and more complex understanding of your research topic. This is because standard textbooks often cover a lot of information, and are therefore not able to go into the depth of detail that an article, a monograph or an edited volume can. By consulting the literature, you are also ensuring that you have the most relevant and up-to-date information on the topic. Scientific knowledge advances constantly, and many good-quality textbooks that are used as core texts on university syllabi are years or even decades old. Using the scientific literature to advance your understanding of a topic can also help you to consider it from a new perspective. For example, a Google Scholar search for 'cancer chemotherapy side effects' currently displays articles about the management of nausea, vomiting and cardiac side effects, but the results also display studies that investigate the patient perception of these side effects, as well as the mental side effects of the therapy – both of which are emerging topics on the issue that are not always considered in textbooks.

Answering a research question

The foundations of a good dissertation lie in the construction of meaningful and well-focused research questions. You should have around three to five research questions that you will tackle throughout your project which will form the direction for your work. You might want to use a concept map, such as the one shown below, to identify the relevant topics and themes that you will need to address during your writing. By breaking down a research question in this way, you will give yourself the subheadings of your literature review chapter, as well as keywords that will be useful in kicking off your literature search.

Considering the example concept map below, we can see that there are two main themes of investigation that the Neuroscience student should follow when searching for literature relating to their research question: mice as analogues in clinical research, and the use of opioid painkillers during childbirth. These, along with the sub-branches of the concept map, will help to guide a focused literature search which will help to answer this specific research question.

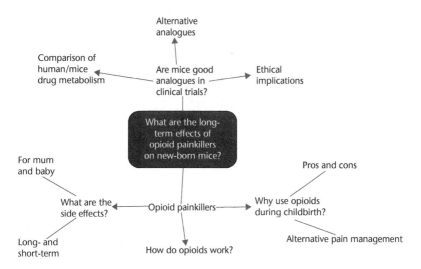

Figure 5   Concept mapping a Neuroscience dissertation research question

Aiding data analysis

Many dissertation discussion chapters do a really good job of fully analysing the results: we find out what the data means and whether the findings answer the research question. This doesn't go far enough, though – remember that by conducting research, you are taking part in the academic conversation (see Chapter 1) and to do that, you need to include the work of others. For a truly complete discussion, the results need to be placed within the context of the scientific literature. Results presented by themselves are weak and unimportant. It is only when you compare your findings with those in the published literature that you begin to add weight to your data.

To guide the search for this literature, it is useful to summarize the following information in four bullet points:

- A summary of the research questions that your dissertation intends to answer. For example, 'What are the long-term effects of opioid painkillers on new-born mice?'
- The protocol you followed to collect your data. For example, 'Fentanyl injected into new-born mice at birth and later. Breathing, stress-indicators and weight were recorded and compared against a control group.'
- Your 'headline results'. For example, 'Adverse effects were observed across all measured variables in fentanyl injected mice.'
- Your main conclusion. For example, 'Exposure to opioid painkillers at birth has a long-term effect on breathing, stress and weight.'

The answers to this five-minute exercise can then be used as a basis for your literature search. For example, if your headline result is 'Adverse effects were observed across all measured variables in fentanyl injected mice', then your search would focus on finding studies that measured the same variables so that a comparison can be made. Before you use the databases as described below, though, go back to your literature review to pick up on the studies that you've already introduced into your dissertation. Analyse these again in the context of your findings by comparing and contrasting results and conclusions.

Beginning the literature search

The process of choosing literature to include in your dissertation looks like a funnel. Initially, you should conduct a broad search, then filter the results until you have a custom-selected set of texts that you can read in depth and include in your dissertation. Here are the steps to curating that selection.

Step 1: Using online databases

Once you identify the topics that you'd like to consider, the next stage is to explore the available literature. Although you could visit the library and look through physical copies of books and journals, it's not recommended as a time-efficient means of sourcing literature. A dissertation can be researched entirely online, although you may need to visit the library if your institution doesn't have electronic copies of a particular article that you'd like to read (this is rare). Three fantastic resources for finding relevant papers are Google Scholar (scholar.google.com), Scopus (scopus.com) and Web of Science (webofknowledge.com). You may, depending on your subject, have access to subject-specific literature databases that collate examples of work in your field, but it's probably best to begin with a Google Scholar search. Although you'll be asked to log in to many journal websites to get access to the articles you find in your literature search, you should have access to electronic journals through your university library. If you find that an article that you're interested in is behind a paywall, do not pay to receive a copy. It may be the case that your library doesn't subscribe to that particular journal, and in that case, ask your supervisor for guidance or look into inter-library loans (although beware that it usually takes a few days to receive articles you request).

Begin your literature search by using the keywords and phrases that you identified while considering what you need to read. You'll probably want to group keywords together to avoid search results that aren't relevant, for example, the term *mice fentanyl breathing* will produce more relevant results than searching these keywords individually. When you receive results, skim through the titles and open any that seem useful in a new tab on your computer. Don't look any further into individual articles at this point – you just want them open for later. Repeat the search process using all of your listed keywords and phrases for one of your topics to begin building a collection of articles, each open on its own tab in your browser. Below is a non-exhaustive example of how you might go about performing keyword searches for the research question, 'What are the long-term effects of opioid painkillers on new-born mice?' Note that similar searches are performed with one or two of the keywords changed at a time. Don't feel you have to write down every search you perform – noting down the keywords is a guiding practice, rather than something that you will report in your dissertation.

You may wish to use advanced search options that are available on many databases. Options to filters results or use Boolean operators (see Table 8) can help avoid returning large amounts of unrelated literature. For example, you may only be interested in the most recent examples of work on a topic,

AND	Includes results that feature multiple keywords to narrow your search	fentanyl AND childbirth
OR	Include results that feature either keyword to broaden your search	fentanyl OR pethidine
NOT	Excludes specific keywords to narrow your results	fentanyl NOT intrathecal
(...)	Parentheses are used to group keywords and statements.	(fentanyl OR pethidine) AND (childbirth OR labour)
*	Asterisks are used to search for variations of a search term. You can truncate words or replace letters in a word with an asterisk	wom*n – will search for women and woman
' ... '	Quotation marks produce results that include the exact phrase within the marks	'minimum local analgesic dose'

Table 8   Boolean operators and search modifiers

so it might be useful to use a date filter to select only work published in the past five years. You may want to exclude results that use a particular method of analysis, for example 'fentanyl, childbirth, labour, pain NOT intrathecal'. Note that Google adds the Boolean operator AND between each word in your search automatically, so 'fentanyl childbirth labour' will search for articles which include the words 'fentanyl AND childbirth AND labour'. You can use the other Boolean operators via the advanced search option. When you've exhausted your search on one database, you'll probably find that you have quite a number of articles to review. At this point, you can begin to sift through your results to exclude any irrelevant literature and identify the articles that will help you shape your literature review.

Step 2: Narrowing down your options

You'll need to filter the articles you have found in the course of your literature search to decide which papers are worth spending time reading in full. Don't make the mistake of reading whole articles at this point; your time is precious, and it can be all too easy to find yourself reading articles that are not directly related to your research. Instead, go through your tabs one by one to remove any duplicate papers that have turned up under different keyword searches. Following that, read the abstract and conclusion sections of each paper and no more. At this point, you should only choose literature that you intend to analyse later. The abstract is a short synopsis of the full paper and should contain a statement of the purpose of the research, the methods used, the headline results and the main conclusions. This should tell you whether the paper is related to your research and give you an idea of how the findings compare to yours (if you have any at that point). The conclusions in a paper will let you know where and how you might fit the reference in your writing. For example, whether you will be able to use it to support an argument, highlight a problem or as a demonstration of work so far on the topic. Once you've reviewed your literature search results for one topic, you might choose to repeat the search-and-filter process for another topic, or you might move on to reading your selected papers in more depth (see Strategies for effective critical reading on page 64).

Step 3: Organizing your literature

As you may have gathered by this point, you will deal with a large amount of literature in the course of writing your dissertation. To avoid ending up with a folder full of articles and book chapters with no idea of why you saved them, you will need to identify a way of managing these resources. Of course, there are several different options and no single option will suit everybody. As long as you consider the issue and have a method of organizing the literature, it doesn't matter if it is one of the systems recommended here or something entirely different.

There are several online and downloadable reference managers that are specifically designed for storing academic literature needed for research. Your institution may recommend a particular manager, or offer to fund a subscription to those managers that charge a fee. There are several advantages to these reference managers and, given that they are specifically designed for organizing online research, they are popular amongst students and professional academics alike. Most reference managers allow you to store, sort and search for your papers, as well as offering help with writing citations and bibliographies. They can be particularly useful if you work across more than one computer (a home laptop and a library PC, for example) as reference managers utilize cloud storage to allow you to access your papers anywhere. There are many different variations to choose from, but Zotero and Mendeley are commonly used by university students (see Table 17 in Chapter 9 for some more recommendations). While reference managers can be extremely helpful when dealing with large amounts of literature, be mindful that you don't completely rely on the software to provide your citations and references. You must proofread your bibliography in particular to ensure that the references are inserted in the correct format.

If you would rather have a simpler and more 'manual' method of managing your literature, you might utilize an Excel spreadsheet. This has the advantage of being completely customizable and adaptable as you progress through your research. You might choose to record journal paper information (title, author, date, etc) across several columns and add information such as which section of your literature review you intend to use the paper and any notes that might help you remember its contents. You'll then be able to use Excel's search and filter functions to manage and organize your literature. If you choose to use a spreadsheet, however, remember that you will not be able to store or pin your papers within the same programme (as you can in many specialist reference managers), so you will need to consider where you plan to store the pdf copies of your journal papers.

Of course, if you want to be really traditional, you could print out paper copies of the papers you intend to include in your dissertation and keep a physical record of the literature. Many students prefer to read from paper rather than from a computer screen, and being able to write notes directly onto the paper can be a significant advantage. Bear in mind, though, that large amounts of printed articles might be difficult to keep track of. A clear filing system will be required to make searching through the literature easy, and the environmental impact of printing large amounts of paper might mean that an electronic approach might be more worthwhile.

Once you have completed a literature search, narrowed down the available options, curated a selection of relevant information and decided how you will organize and store it, it is time to begin reading in depth.

Strategies for effective critical reading

Reading with a critical and questioning eye is the key to effective reading for your dissertation. You may have completed critical reviews of a topic or a paper as part of your course before you reached your research project, and you'll need to draw on the skills you learned during these assessments when reading for your dissertation.

Keep in mind:

When we refer to critical reading or critical analysis, we are talking about weighing the evidence that is presented to us in the text. What are the strengths and weaknesses of the work, and what can we learn from it as a result?

Ultimately, when you read for your dissertation, you are looking to find evidence for and against your own scientific arguments, as well as to further your own understanding of your research topic. Your initial search and filtering of literature will probably have given you some ideas as to how you'll construct the arguments in your literature review or where certain papers might fit within your discussion chapter. It is important, however, to begin your in-depth critical analysis of the literature with an open and unbiased mind. Don't ever be tempted to form an opinion and then search through your resources to try to find a paper to back up your argument – this is not only unethical, but it will probably be spotted by the person marking your dissertation. Successful students form informed academic opinions (or hypotheses) based on their preliminary reading, and then test these hypotheses using their own data in conjunction with evidence from the literature.

Reading an article vs. reading around a topic

Below are two models of critical reading. One model is suited to analysing the strengths and weaknesses of an individual article. The second model is designed to help you analyse the literature contained in several articles in a topical or thematic way. You will need to use both models of critical analysis during your dissertation writing to present both the breadth and the depth of your knowledge of your research topic. Knowing which type of analysis you will need to report in your writing will help to guide your reading.

Model 1: Critically reading an article

There will be times in your dissertation when it will be appropriate to discuss a particular article or study in depth, for example, to highlight a gap in our knowledge that your dissertation will address, or to compare your study to one with a similar research question. Unlike focusing your critical reading around a topic, where you'll gather evidence from a variety of sources to strengthen a point you'd like to emphasize, individual critical analysis looks at a single body of work. Your reading, therefore, will cover less material, but involve in-depth evaluation.

An individual article analysis requires you to read and question almost every part of the paper. Read and note your analysis of each section of the paper as you go. The guide below will help you to think about the kinds of questions that you should ask about each section, but as you read through the study, always ask yourself whether you are convinced by what the author is telling you. Take an unbiased approach and look for the strengths as well as the weaknesses in the work.

Reading each section of a paper

Abstract

Don't worry about critically analysing the abstract in a scientific paper. You will have read the abstract when deciding whether the paper was relevant to your dissertation, but once you have chosen to include it, there is no need to read it critically.

Introduction

The introduction to a journal article or book chapter sets up the research that is being reported. It should give some background information to the topic, before discussing the aims of the research. Questions you might ask at this stage are:

- Is there a clearly identified research question/s?
- Is the research well justified?
- Are all the claims made backed up by a range of credible sources?

Method

This section of the paper may be difficult to analyse if you are unfamiliar with the protocol that was used. You may need to employ a bit of background reading to be able to understand the methods used. When reading the methods, consider:

- Is the protocol clear and reproducible?
- Does the author use a standard procedure? Is any modification of the standard procedure explained?
- Are adequate sampling strategies used?
- Are appropriate statistical tests described?

Results

Take some time to examine the raw data in the results section and come to your own conclusion about what they describe before you read the author's interpretation. This allows you to analyse the data with a fresh (and unbiased) pair of eyes. Think about:

- Are the data reported clearly and in full?
- Are any omissions in data fully explained?
- Are descriptive statistics presented if required?
- What do you think the data shows?

Discussion

This section should offer a full and fair interpretation of the data in relation to the research question/s identified in the paper's introduction. This is the part of the paper that you can focus a lot of your critical analysis. Ask yourself:

- Are all of the research questions answered using the data presented?
- If there are some questions that remain unanswered, is there an explanation provided for this? Note that not every study will be able to answer all of their research questions, but as long as the reason is clear, it is not necessarily a flaw in the study.
- Is the interpretation of the data balanced and unbiased?

- Do you agree with the interpretation of the data?
- Do any of the findings seem exaggerated?
- Are the limitations of the data identified?
- How is the data discussed within the context of the wider literature?

Conclusion

The conclusion of the paper should summarize the headline findings of the paper without offering any new interpretations of the data. You might ask:

- Are the findings of the study realistic and backed up by solid evidence?
- What are the considerations for further research following the study?

Bibliography

There's no need to look up every paper that is cited within a journal article; however, you can make some interesting observations by reading through the reference list at the end of a paper.

- Is there an extensive bibliography which suggests that the author has used a wide range of evidence to back up their arguments?
- Do they cite mainly other journal articles (rather than books or websites) to show that they are familiar with the work in their field?
- Do they cite a lot of their own work, rather than discussing that of other academics?

Taking notes for an individual paper analysis

There are a couple of effective note-taking options to consider when critically analysing individual articles. You may choose to make notes directly on the article itself. This method allows you to highlight specific parts of the text, make notes directly on figures and has the advantage of keeping both your notes and the article in one place (either physically or electronically). A disadvantage of noting directly onto an article is space restriction. While you might be able to use the margins or spaces between sections to record your analysis, it does not afford a lot of room for in-depth comments. If you would prefer to be unrestricted by space constraints, you might consider keeping your notes in a separate document, formatted in the layout shown above (i.e. with your analysis of each section of the paper defined with headings). There is also a growing variety of software specifically designed to help you make and organize notes, from the most simple forms, such as Adobe pdf editor and Apple notes, to the more complex programmes that could help to organize your entire project, such as Evernote and Microsoft OneNote. Your university may be able to recommend or even supply note-taking apps for you to use during your dissertation: your IT department or library is usually a good place to start with the hunt for free software.

Model 2: Reading around a topic

To illustrate reading literature on a particular topic, we'll continue to consider the subject of the effects of opioid painkillers on new-born mice. Related to this topic is the efficacy of different opioid painkillers. A focused and relevant question to guide a thematic analysis would be, 'How effective is fentanyl compared to pethidine as pain relief during labour?'

Step 1: Identify a topic

For critical reading around a particular topic or theme, you will need to gather the papers you have identified from your literature search on a topic and then begin to consider your thread of investigation: what do you want to know from these papers? You need to use your time wisely, and therefore avoid reading aimlessly. Reading every paper on a topic will give you a really good idea of the work that's been carried out on that subject, but you're unlikely to have much of an idea of how you'll write about that work. Instead, think about what you need to know to be able to write your literature review (or whichever section of your dissertation you're working on), and look through your selection of literature for that specific information. By focusing your reading in this way, you will save valuable time and probably find yourself more motivated to read. You may end up finding useful information on something else that is relevant to your research; in this situation make a note to come back to the paper at a later time and try to avoid going off on a tangent, otherwise you'll lose the focus of your reading.

Step 2: Collate the evidence

With one or two questions in mind to direct you, you can then begin to read your selected literature to answer these questions. When reading literature on a topic, it is okay to scan the paper you're reading to get a fair understanding of the content, but without doing an in-depth analysis of every section. If, for example, you're looking to find out what academics in your field have found in relation to the efficacy of intravenous opioids on the management of labour pain, there is little point in scrutinizing the introduction of every paper on the topic. Instead, scan the article to get your bearings and then concentrate on picking apart the relevant results. Note that this approach to reading is not effective for critically analysing an individual article (model 1), where in-depth analysis of all parts of a paper

Paper reference	Evidence
Fleet et al. (2016)	Fentanyl faster acting and has fewer side effects
Hutchison et al. (2006)	Lower pain scores and fewer adverse reactions for fentanyl
Fleet, Jones and Belan (2017)	Fentanyl elicited more positive effects than pethidine. Intranasal fentanyl was more effective than subcutaneous

Table 9   Use of fentanyl vs. pethidine for pain relief during labour

is necessary. For each paper that you read to critically evaluate a topic or theme, make a note of the evidence you find in relation to your question (see the example table above) – you will quickly begin to build a larger picture of the evidence available on the topic you're interested in which spans the body of literature in your subject.

Step 3: Weigh the evidence
While it is a great start to have a range of different theories, results and statistics from several papers to back up your writing, it is not the end of the critical analysis process. To create a sophisticated argument, you should also take into account the strength of your evidence, not just that the evidence exists. You may, for example, have made a note of two studies that you have identified to back up the argument that the administration of fentanyl to new-born mice will affect their response to the same drug administered later in their lifespan. It will not be enough, however, to make a statement to that effect in your literature review and then provide the citations to the two studies. The studies may make these conclusions, but their conclusions may be based on poor-quality research or limited data. You must, therefore, also make a statement about the quality of the evidence to further strengthen your argument.

Considering the evidence

The process of weighing up academic evidence is very similar to the process of weighing evidence in a criminal court. Different sources of evidence have differing values; for example, an audio-visual recording of a robbery would be considered stronger evidence than an eye-witness testimony. However, you must consider not only the *source* of the evidence but also the *type* of evidence. An example of this is comparing a high-definition mobile phone recording of the robbery to grainy CCTV footage of the same event.

Figure 6   The hierarchy of scientific evidence

When considering the type of evidence you're examining, you may want to consider where the evidence sits in the hierarchy of evidence, particularly if you are studying a subject that involves clinical literature. Figure 6 shows this hierarchy as a pyramid, with studies that are designed to reduce risk of bias sitting at the top, and the risk of bias increasing as you look down the pyramid. It's worth noting that is isn't necessary to only use evidence found at the top of the hierarchy pyramid. For example, professional opinion does have a place in scientific research, but if you include it, acknowledge that it is opinion and not peer-reviewed and therefore not necessarily accepted by the wider scientific community.

This hierarchy isn't relevant to all subjects, so don't worry if you don't recognize the types of evidence shown in the pyramid. The indicators of good-quality research will vary according to your field. What makes good research in environmental science, for example, might not even be a factor that is considered in a physics study, so as well as following the advice in this book, it's important that you also think about what makes good research in your subject. When judging the quality of the evidence you have gathered, you might want to consider the following questions:

1. How relevant is the study to your statement? This question is a judgement of how well the evidence fits your statement, rather than a judgement of how good the research you're reading is. If a paper you're interested in has investigated the same research question as you, but (for example) has applied it to a different location or population, you can point out their findings and note that it may be possible to predict an outcome to your research based on the paper in question, but that the differences between your study and theirs justifies your research.

2. Is the study well designed? Every study published in a scientific journal should follow a reproducible method that is designed to measure the intended variables, whilst also limiting confounding factors. The method should also be fair and unbiased, meaning that there should not be a chance that the authors could have influenced the study outcome. Finally, if the study tests a sample to extrapolate the data to a population, the sample must be representative and a good size.
3. Are the conclusions sensible? For a study to be credible, it must be realistic in its reporting of findings. The conclusions to a good study should be based on a reasonable and unbiased interpretation of the data, and include a statement of the limitations of the research. If the conclusions seem to be sensationalized, over-reaching or go beyond the scope of the results, it would be fair to question their practicality.

Consider the three questions above when weighing up the value of your evidence and make a note of your conclusions. In the example in Table 10, a column has been added to the earlier information shown in table 9 to include some analysis of the evidence. Note that there are both positive and negative judgements of the literature. Many students make the mistake of only looking for the weaknesses in the scientific literature, but a well-rounded critical analysis includes both positive and negative criticism. Don't worry if you find that the evidence you read varies in quality. You will rarely come across a single, gold standard journal article that will perfectly back up a point in your writing. Instead, you will find that you need to use the weight of several different studies together to build a strong scientific argument.

Paper reference	Evidence	Analysis of Evidence
Fleet et al. (2016)	Fentanyl faster acting and has fewer side effects.	Randomized-controlled trial – high-quality primary research.
Hutchison et al. (2006)	Lower pain scores and fewer adverse reactions for fentanyl.	Looked at post-operative analgesia, not labour – not directly relevant to my research.
Fleet, Jones and Belan (2017)	Fentanyl elicited more positive effects than pethidine. Intranasal fentanyl was more effective than subcutaneous.	Unclear whether increased mobility that fentanyl allows was a factor for pain management.

Table 10   Critical analysis of evidence for efficacy of fentanyl vs. pethidine for pain relief during labour

Keeping notes on the literature you have read for your dissertation doesn't have to look exactly as the examples given in this book. You may adapt or customize these notes as you see fit. The important thing, however, is that **you must make notes as you read**. There is nothing more frustrating than writing a really solid section of your literature review, and then finding that you're unable to find the references to go along with your argument. Taking notes as you read may seem like extra work at the time; however, you are more likely to stay focused on your topic, be more motivated to continue reading and you'll save time during the writing stage when you use the notes to structure your arguments.

Final word on critical reading

Keep in mind that as you read and analyse the literature you've selected, you will very likely come across other papers that maybe didn't turn up in your initial database search. This method of research is called backwards citation tracing or chain searching. Look for studies that authors cite and discuss in the introduction sections of articles and look through the bibliographies of each paper for any potential work you might have missed. This technique can be used to find the origins of a theory or protocol, or to trace the development and applications of scientific work through time.

Reading critically in science takes time, but it is a skill that becomes easier to do the more you practice. Reading journal articles at the beginning of your research project might seem like a laborious task, but you'll improve in your ability to critically analyse scientific work as you progress through your work. The golden rule that *always* applies when reading scientific literature is to be unbiased. Never go looking for a paper to fit a preconceived opinion, and equally, don't exclude something you've read just because it doesn't fit your narrative. Finally, at some point, every student finds an article that seems so close to your dissertation that it seems like the work has already been done. Don't panic! Simply look carefully through the research questions asked and methods used to find the difference between the paper and your project (it will be there). Then make sure to include that paper in your literature review, and discuss how your work is complementary/distinct. You will hopefully end up with a large collection of notes from your time spent reading. The next chapter will show you how to turn these notes into the most important chapters of your dissertation.

Next steps

	Define your reason for reading the literature (e.g. literature review, discussion, introduction)
	Determine whether you will need to read around a topic or complete a single article analysis
	Decide on your note-taking strategy
	Explore the range of subject-specific databases in your field of study

Using evidence in your dissertation

Introduction

All scientific knowledge is based on evidence collected from various sources. No claim in STEM is considered valid until it is backed up by sufficient evidence, and this extends to your research as a student as well. This chapter covers three types of evidence: published literature, your own data and visual evidence.

Topics in this chapter include:

- Using the academic literature to build a scientific argument
- Using language to hone your arguments
- Presenting your data as evidence
- Showing the trends within your data
- Using other visual tools as evidence in your research.

What academic rules do I need to consider when writing about literature?

After the practical part of your project is complete, you'll need to knuckle down to writing the report. As you might expect, there are good practice principles to consider in your writing. You will no doubt be aware of the risks of plagiarizing in your degree work, but what do you need to consider to avoid plagiarism in research? All universities have individual rules on plagiarism, but collectively, higher education and academic strongly condemns those who break them. Your university should have guidance on their plagiarism policy and this is usually available on their website. Make it a priority to know where the guidance is and to understand the rules. If you are accused of plagiarism, you may be penalized by your university if found guilty and, unfortunately, it doesn't matter whether you committed the offence knowingly or accidentally. There's a full chapter in this book dedicated to avoiding plagiarism (Chapter 9), but a summary of this is below.

Broadly speaking, plagiarism is defined as attempting to pass off someone else's work as your own; this could be published research or your friend's work – it doesn't matter. There are two ways to avoid plagiarism in your dissertation:

1. Always make it explicit when you use external sources in your research. You should be extensively drawing on external sources, usually from journal papers, in your dissertation. You will use these sources as evidence to support your own theories, arguments or interpretations. It is vitally important that you make it clear when you are writing about your own ideas and research and when you are referring to evidence from published studies. You can ensure this by providing a citation in the correct place after each source that you discuss. Chapter 9 has in-depth guidance, with examples, on how to choose and use the correct referencing system for your dissertation. The key rule to referencing, though, is always refer to the original source of the information.

2. Complete your written work alone. Your dissertation is an individual research project. As such, working with others to write your report would be considered collusion; this is a form of plagiarism where students work in pairs or groups when completing individual assessments. The thinking behind prohibiting collusion is that you should earn the grade you deserve. If your dissertation gets an A grade, but you don't fully understand some of the discussion chapter because a classmate helped you to write it, then you can't claim that you earned that A. If you ever have any questions about your dissertation research, your supervisor should be your first stop. Of course, you will probably discuss your work with friends and classmates and they may even help you to understand certain concepts in your project; that is absolutely fine, as long as you are the one that explains those concepts in your dissertation at the end of it all.

Academic literature as evidence

Being able to discuss and incorporate external evidence from published literature into your writing is a key part of academic research. A scientific study in isolation is of little use until it is placed within the context of the literature to demonstrate what it changes and how it adds to knowledge about a subject. Knowing how to structure an argument, strengthen it with external evidence and use your choice of language to frame your academic views will result in a sophisticated and valuable piece of research. In addition to this, understanding how to strengthen the credibility of your data using references to other people's work, and knowing how to deal with instances where your findings disagree with the literature, will increase the integrity of your work.

Constructing a scientific argument

Constructing a convincing scientific argument requires you to have come to a conclusion about what your stance is before you start writing. This means that you have read all of the relevant literature on the topic and you know in advance what evidence you will present to back up your claims. Arguments constructed as you write are never as effective at convincing the reader as those that are considered beforehand. Whenever you are writing critically in your report, make a bullet point plan that sets out your claim/s and evidence so that you can make sure that you present your argument in a logical order and that you have included all of the evidence you need to.

Important!

If you include a citation in your writing without directly discussing the work, you still need to have fully read and evaluated the work, as detailed in Chapter 6. Don't skip the evaluation just because you're not writing it down. Including references to papers you have only skim-read risks using poor-quality research as evidence in your report, or misinterpreting information because you haven't properly read the paper.

Using a well-considered structure when making your arguments and claims will help to guide the reader through your thought process and make your writing clear and comprehensible. Note that a full and in-depth study of a paper isn't always required; the suggested structure on p 77 is to be used for constructing complex and in-depth scientific arguments. The choice to present an in-depth, structured summary and analysis of a citation should be based on the point you're making in your writing and how much the source contributes to your argument. There will be many times that you will need to cite a source because the information you write can be attributed to a particular paper. If the source is not essential to the argument you are making, however, it would be irrelevant and confusing to your reader if you were to go into a detailed evaluation about that source.

Constructing an argument using the literature

Claim
- Make your thesis statement
- What is the point or argument that you will unpack in the rest of the paragraph?
- Use straightforward and concise language so that your reader is certain of your position before you present the evidence

Present the evidence
- Cite one or more papers that support your claim
- Think about your use of language here, 'this claim is backed up by ...' 'Smith et al. (1999) supports this with ...' etc.
- Paraphrase the information within the paper that is relevent to your claim

Evaluate the evidence
- Show why the evidence you have presented is good quality
- The strength of the evidence might come from a large sample, size, a robust method, some conclusive data, or from many studies that all agree with each other
- Discuss any potential limitations of the evidence

Link evidence and claim
- Show why the evidence supports your claim
- Don't let your reader assume the connection – be specific
- You may need to combine information from several sources to make the link

Discuss counter-evidence
- Don't ignore any papers that disagree with your claim (where these exist)
- Present the counter-claim/s and discuss their value as evidence
- Incorporate some caution to your claim if necessary

Conclusion or link to next paragraph
- Wrap up your argument by showing the reader that the evidence supports the claim
- You might also make a reference to the next argument you'll present if it is closely related to the one you're concluding

Using language to convince your reader

You can use the suggested structure above to construct a huge variety of scientific arguments. You might argue in favour of a claim made by you or another author, you might dispute a claim made in the literature and you might even argue that something is unclear, and needs further investigation before a solid conclusion can be made. You might even state that your claim isn't even an argument, and that it is actually an accepted feature of your subject that is backed up by many different sources. There

Increasing certainty			
It could be the case that ...	The evidence indicates ...	It is probable that ...	It is widely accepted that ...
Possibly	Suggests	Tends to be	Certainly
May/might	Points towards	It is likely/unlikely	Absolutely
Smith (2021) claims that	Could be attributed to	It is reasonable that	Without a doubt

Table 11   Examples of hedging language used in academic writing

are many subtle intricacies involved in putting a scientific argument together, and your use of language can help to convey these complexities to your reader.

The best scientific arguments are those that are clear and direct. When discussing evidence, be explicit when explaining why it is good or poor quality and how it links to your claim; don't just describe the evidence and expect your reader to make the conclusions about why it is useful. When making a claim or a conclusion, hedging language is extremely useful at indicating the strength of a claim or a piece of evidence, and is a linguistic device that should be built into your discussion of the literature. Some examples of hedging can be found in the Table 11.

Your tone and use of persuasive language will also have a direct effect on how convincing your writing is. In the sciences, objectivity is key to credibility, and this must be conveyed in your tone and word choice. Always convey your academic opinion, which is backed up by external evidence, and not your personal opinion which may be subjective. To avoid introducing personal opinion and emotive language into your writing, steer clear of 'I think' and other phrases that use the first-person narrative. Instead, make the focus of your writing on what the evidence shows. See the example in Exercise 3 for a demonstration of correct tone.

Exercise 3: The building blocks of a scientific argument

The following paragraph is a model scientific argument that uses all the linguistic techniques discussed above to demonstrate their effectiveness. Read the example and try to identify all the techniques. Underneath the paragraph is a list of the techniques employed. Check whether you spotted them all and try to identify any that you missed.

Though the isotopic evidence for a rapid change in diet at the Mesolithic-Neolithic transition is clear, there are few other methods which back up its claims. Stable isotope analysis is the most commonly used and valuable methods of recreating diet; however, analysis of bone collagen reconstructs long term dietary habits over the 5–10 years prior to death, depending on which bone is sampled (Sealy et al. 1995; Richards and Hedges 1999). This means that minor or periodic contributions of marine resources to a dominantly terrestrial diet (and vice versa) are not detectable in the data. It would be reasonable to expect that other sources of evidence would exist to back up the stable isotope results, though. While the analysis of lipid biomarkers and stable isotope analysis of pot residue has shown that dairying replaced fishing in the Neolithic, this method of analysis is limited because it only takes into account one method of cooking (Cramp et al. 2014). Meat and fish can be baked in pit ovens, cooked on heated slabs or roasted over a fire, so we can only say that this method shows that dairy products replaced fish in meals cooked in pots. The statistical analysis of archaeozoology from multiple sites across Europe has indicated that Neolithic communities chose sites that were conducive to agricultural activity rather than hunting (Manning et al. 2013). This supports the argument that farming was far more important to Neolithic people than hunting but doesn't disprove the notion of occasional or opportunistic hunting and fishing.

The above paragraph includes:

- A transition that links the previous paragraph with the upcoming argument (this technique is discussed in Chapter 8, pages 121 and 122 of this book).
- Claims that require a citation, but don't require an evaluation of the source.
- A direct discussion of literature, including a summary of the research and an evaluation of its credibility as evidence.
- Clear, logical progression between the claim and the conclusion.
- A demonstration of the link between the evidence and the claim in the argument.
- An objective tone.
- Demonstration of various degrees of hedging.

Presenting data as evidence

Your collected data is one of the most important pieces of evidence in your research because it is a demonstration of your contribution to the topic. Your data will be entirely new and unique. By design, your data will be derived from samples never measured before, or never measured to address the research question you are asking in your research. The way that you visually present your evidence will impact its effectiveness as evidence: clearly and correctly presented data will aid the reader in understanding how it relates to your research question.

For all visual data, no matter what the format, there are two conventions that should always be followed:

1. Have a descriptive caption
   Each table, graph or other figure should have a numbered caption (positioned above tables and below figures and graphs) so that you can refer readers to the information in your writing. Captions should fully describe the contents of the table and include any references if you have adapted a table or included data from elsewhere. In Microsoft Word, captions can be added using the Captions tool (References > Insert Caption) and using this feature will make adding a list of figures and tables easier as Word will automatically compile this for you (References > Insert Table of Figures). A list of figures and a list of tables should be inserted after the table of contents in dissertations. Shorter report may not require this, and it is at your discretion to add these lists if you feel they would be helpful to the reader.

2. Refer to the information in your text
   Always point your readers towards tables at appropriate times in your writing. You should never have a table in your report that you don't refer to in the text. Examples of language to use here are, 'Table 1 shows data collected in November 2019' or 'As can be seen in Figure 2, the measurements ranged between 20.3 and 26.9 cm.'

Presenting data in tables

If you are dealing with quantitative data, you must present this in its raw numerical form before you begin manipulating it to reveal trends and patterns. This is to ensure your findings are replicable and to allow other researchers to use your data in answering their own research questions. All measured data must be calibrated and normalized (if appropriate) and then presented in tables in the results section of your report. There are a few rules to follow when putting tables together to make sure that they are clear and logically presented.

1. Think about column and row headers
   You can choose the order in which you present data in your tables, and you should always consider this when designing tables for your report. Tables are often initially read from left to right, so keep this in mind when thinking about the order of your column headers. It makes sense, for example, to have key identifying information such as sample names or locations as the first column headers, rather than having the data measurements in this first position. You may, once you have initially designed your table, wish to swap around columns and rows to present the information in the most logical format. Don't forget to include any relevant units of measurement in brackets in headers.

2. Think about orientation
   Tables do not have to be orientated in portrait. If you have many columns of information that won't fit onto the page, consider presenting your table in landscape. To format a table in landscape, insert a section break before and after your table (Layout > Page Setup > Breaks), then change the orientation of the table to landscape (Layout > Orientation > Landscape). This will move your table to a separate landscape page, but keep the rest of your work in portrait.

3. Try to avoid having tables that break over multiple pages
   Often when reading tables, we compare data across different columns and rows. For this reason, it is best if you can avoid positioning your table so that it splits across two or more pages. This may result in a gap on the page between the table and the text, but this is still preferable to splitting your table. Of course, there may be times when your data won't physically fit onto the page without making the font smaller. In this case, split the table but ensure that the header row is repeated at the top of the table on each page.

As well as presenting all numerical data in tables, you may also choose to summarize some text-based information in a table rather than in the body of your report. The example below follows all of the rules outlined above when presenting text-based information. In the example (Table 12), taken from Bownes (2018), information about samples are summarized for the reader. Presenting text in this way is a good way to highlight important information in a clear and concise way. Had this information been included in the text as opposed to a table, it would probably have been very difficult to follow.

Sample ID	Species	Site
GU-36227	Wildcat (*Felis silvestris*)	Loch Borralie, Durness
GUsi-3482	Lynx (*Lynx lynx*)	Loch Borralie, Durness
GUsi-3483	Lynx (*Lynx lynx*)	Loch Borralie, Durness
GUsi-3484	Wolf (*Canis lupus*)	Loch Borralie, Durness
GUsi-3485	Roe deer (*Capreolus capreolus*)	Risga, Loch Sunart
GUsi-3486	Red deer (*Cervus elaphus*)	Risga, Loch Sunart
GUsi-3492	Red deer (*Cervus elaphus*)	Risga, Loch Sunart
GUsi-3493	Red deer (*Cervus elaphus*)	Risga, Loch Sunart
GUsi-3494	Red deer (*Cervus elaphus*)	Risga, Loch Sunart
GUsi-3495	Pig (*Sus scrofa*)	Risga, Loch Sunart
GUsi-3496	Pig (*Sus scrofa*)	Risga, Loch Sunart
GUsi-3497	medium mammal (*Ovis aries* or *Capreolus capreolus*)	Carding Mill Bay, Oban

Table 12   An example of summary information about samples in a table (adapted from Bownes, J., 2018. Reassessing the Scottish Mesolithic-Neolithic transition: questions of diet and chronology (Doctoral dissertation, University of Glasgow)

Remember that tables summarize information only. They do not show evidence of trends, patterns or relationships you have found; each of these must be presented by a figure or a statistical test.

Presenting data in graphs

Once you have laid out all of your data in tables in the results section of your report, you can begin to use that information to answer your research questions in the discussion section. You should have decided in advance of your data collection what relationships you are looking for, so you should already have a good idea of the type and number of graphs you will need to design for your report. When deciding to display your data in graphs, think carefully about the trend you would like to highlight; each graph should show one trend, meaning you may need multiple graphs to adequately discuss all the data you have collected.

The first step to designing graphs is to choose the correct type of graph for your data. The most common types of graphs and their uses are summarized in Table 13.

Graph type	Suitable data/trend	Tips
Scatter plot	Used to show the relationship between multiple individual measurements. Can be used to identify relationships between variables, distribution of data and to help identify outliers.	If you use a trend line to show a positive or negative corellation in your data, remember to display the r value and the equation for the line to aid statistical analysis in your writing.
Line graph	Used to show multiple measurements of continuous data. Can be used to identify changes over time.	If you are plotting more than one line on the same graph, make sure that each line is clearly distinguishable from the others.
Bar chart	Used to compare the frequency of categorical data. Data are plotted into discrete (separate) horizontal or vertical bars.	Think about what the logical order of the bars should be on the x axis.
Histogram	Used to compare the frequency of numerical data. Data are plotted into continuous (touching) bars.	Data should be organized into intervals before it is plotted in the graph.
Pie chart	Shows the percentage composition of a whole that has been split up into categories. The categories can be visually compared between each other.	The 'slices' of a pie chart should add up to 100% and make each slice a different colour to aid data interpretation. Label each slice with their percentage value.

Table 13   Common graph types used in research

As with tables, there are some rules to putting good-quality graphs together.

1. Include all labels

   Every graph should be properly labelled so that the reader can interpret the data without needing to refer to the text in your report. As a minimum, graphs should have descriptive axis labels (that include units of measurement where appropriate), and a key if there is more than one dataset displayed.

2. Think about axis scale

   Not all graphs need to have axes that begin at zero. For a scatter plot, for example, it might be better to begin the x and/or y axis at a value greater than zero to ensure your data don't get squashed up into one corner of the plot area.

3. Think about unit increments

When including unit increments on the x or y axis of a graph, think about what increment makes the data easily interpretable and the visual appearance of the increment labels of the axes. Avoid having too large a space between increments so that data points are difficult to read, and too small increments so that the increment markers look squashed up on the axes.

4. Think about use of colour

If you use multiple colours in the same graph, consider the contrast between the colours if they are printed in black and white – will they still be distinguishable? Also avoid using colours such as red and green, which are not visible to people with colour blindness.

Presenting data using statistics

Using statistics to show relationships, patterns and trends in your data can be a powerful tool when addressing your research questions. Being able to prove that the relationship between two variables is statistically significant adds a wealth of credibility to your findings. It can be very easy to misuse statistics, however, accidentally or otherwise. It is important, therefore, to choose the correct test for the data you have, and to be transparent with your results.

When deciding on the correct test to apply to your data, you must consider the type of data you have and the questions you want to ask of your data. It can be very tempting to collect data and see if you notice any patterns in the raw results, then decide on statistical tests to run based on your initial observations. This approach, however, is not ethically sound as it introduces bias into the test before you even run it. For this reason, you should think about what statistical approach you want to take on your data before you collect it: are you looking for differences between groups within a population, or distributions or correlations? All of these investigations require different tests and different types of data, so thinking about this before the data collection stage will help you collect the most relevant data for your research. Below is a summary of common statistical tests that can be applied to answer different questions about data. This is not an exhaustive list, and it is strongly recommended that you are very familiar with the statistical tests you intend to use in your research. Your supervisor can help you decide on which tests are most appropriate and can guide you to resources to help you learn more about how to apply these tests.

Statistical test	What this test shows	Purpose of test	Data required
Mean	Central tendency	To find the average value of the dataset	A set of continuous values
Median	Central tendency	To find the middle value in a dataset	A set of skewed continuous values OR a set of ordinal categorical data
Mode	Central tendency	To find the most frequently occurring value	A set of nominal categorical data
Standard deviation	Distribution	To show the variability of the data	A set of normally distributed continuous values
Standard error	Distribution	To find the uncertainty of a calculated mean value	A set of normally distributed continuous values
Independent t-test	Comparison	To investigate whether there is a difference between the in the mean values of two potentially related groups of data	Two sets of continuous values. There are different tests for paired and unpaired data
ANOVA	Comparison	To investigate whether there is a difference between the mean values of three or more potentially related groups of data	Two or more sets of continuous values or categorical data
Chi-square	Association	To investigate whether two variables are related	Two or more groups of independent categorical data
Simple linear regression	Association	To investigate the relationship between two variables	Measurements of an independent and a dependant quantitative variable

Table 14   Common statistical tests used to find trends in quantitative data

As well as selecting the correct test for your data and your research, there are some standards to keep in mind when working with statistics:

1. Report all results, even if they turn out to be not significant.
    It can be tempting to omit the results of statistical tests that do not support the claim you want to make. Results like this may be difficult to explain; however, for obvious reasons, it is highly unethical to ignore

statistical results that don't support your hypothesis. Once you have committed to a test and you are confident that the results will be valid, the best course of action is to be objectively informed by the outcome. This means that if the results don't support your argument, you should report them anyway. You have two options in this case: if you have enough other evidence that supports your claim, you can present this alongside the statistical results and combine these to make a suitably cautious argument, or you can amend your argument. You should always be guided by the evidence, and if the statistical evidence supports a counter-claim, this must be discussed.

2. If your results include a p-value, be clear on what this means.
   In inferential statistics, the aim is to make conclusions about a population based on the findings of your measurements of a sample from that population. These tests produce a p-value (probability value) that can be used to make statements about how statistically significant the test findings are. P-values are commonly misinterpreted, however, reducing the credibility of any claims that are made that use p-values as evidence. P-values do not prove or disprove the hypothesis you test; they don't even indicate the probability of your findings being correct (as many students and professionals believe). A statistically significant p-value ($p > 0.05$) indicates that there is a less than 5 per cent chance of finding the same observed relationship in the data in repeated studies if the null hypothesis was true. This is evidence to suggest that the alternative hypothesis is acceptable. This holds a different weight to the more common interpretation of p-values, so ensure that you use the correct definition and the correct amount of caution when assessing p-values as evidence.

3. Report all of the relevant information.
   When reporting statistical results, there is a minimum amount of information that you must report. For descriptive statistics, this information is simply a measure of central tendency (mean, median or mode) and the distribution (standard deviation or standard error). For inferential statistics, there is more required information and you might consider showing this information in a table or some of the information in an appendix if you are running many tests of this type. The information you should report for inferential statistics is:

   - The null and the alternative hypothesis
   - The test statistic value (e.g. t value for a t-test or the f value for ANOVA)
   - Degrees of freedom (the number of values in a calculation that are free to vary)
   - P-value (see the definition above).

4. Get training and be confident in using your chosen package before you run your tests.

   Statistics are complex. For statistical tests to be accurate, they must be chosen carefully, calculated using the correct information and reported fully. When calculating inferential statistics, specialist software such as MATLAB, R or SPSS are often utilized. To ensure that your statistics are accurate, it is essential that you fully understand your data, the tests you are using and any tools you employ. For this reason, many institutions require students to undertake specific modules in data handling and/or statistics prior to the beginning of any dissertation. If you are not fully confident in applying statistics in your research, ask your supervisor for support or direction to training and advice. YouTube is also a valuable resource for tutorials and walk-throughs.

Using other visual evidence

Aside from literature and your own data, there is a wealth of other visual aids that you can employ as evidence in your research. These range from photographs and maps, for example to evidence the original location of samples, to diagrams and infographics, as evidence of the origin of a design or the design method. Each of these forms of evidence should be used according to certain guidelines to ensure the credibility of the information you show.

Copyright protection

If you want to use a piece of visual evidence in your research that you did not produce yourself, you must check the copyright permissions associated with the image. In the UK, images are automatically protected by copyright law which prevents people from copying or adapting the work. This means that the person who produced the image doesn't need to apply for the protection or display anything alongside their work to be protected. This can make using images in research complicated. The basic rules to follow to avoid copyright infringement are:

1. Seek permission from the image owner to use the image in your work. This can be as simple as sending an email request to the owner if you have their details. Note that you might be asked for payment in return for the use of an image. In this case, consider how important the image is for your research, think about whether an alternative can be used and, if the image is essential, ask your supervisor about funding to pay for the copyright permission instead of paying for this yourself.

2. Look for images that are copyright free. Many images are copyright free because the owner has granted permission for the work to be shared. These types of images can be found using the Creative Commons database (https://creativecommons.org/) or by using the Usage Rights filter tool in Google Images. These images should be credited to their owner (as should all work you include in your research that is not your own) but you don't need to seek permission to use them.
3. If you are struggling to find a copyright-free image that you know will be helpful in your report, consider whether this is something you can produce yourself. The brief guides below outline the minimum standards expected of visual evidence in academic research.

Photographs

Many academic subjects that rely on the use of photography in the production of research have published guidelines on the standards that should be followed when recording samples and locations using photographs. Your supervisor will be able to direct you to the relevant guidelines if this is a feature of your subject. If no specific guidelines are available, the following should be taken into account:

1. Gain permission from any subjects you wish to feature or from the owner of any private locations you wish to photograph.
2. Use the best-quality equipment you can source. There is no need to purchase equipment yourself and many institutions have cameras and lighting equipment for students to borrow for their research.
3. Think about resolution and lighting. The aim of photography in academic research is to accurately record an image. This means that the image should be clear, not blurry, and well-lit so that the appropriate amount of detail can be seen. If you are a novice, the automatic focus options on the camera you are using will be useful. Natural light is often best for photographs, but make sure that it is not so bright that it washes out any detail you want to record. Additional lighting may be required; any lighting you use should be evenly distributed across the subject.
4. Use photographic scales where appropriate. Scales are used to show the viewer the size and orientation of photographed objects. Specialist scales are available, but a ruler or metre stick can easily be used to show size and a printed arrow on A4 paper can indicate the location of North.
5. Avoid using a photograph just because it looks pretty. This rule is true of all visual evidence in academic research, but it is particularly tempting to include an impressive photograph because it is aesthetically pleasing. Every photograph in your report should have a clear purpose, convey information to the viewer and add something tangible to your work.

Maps

Not all subjects and research projects will use maps, but where you decide to use them, there are some standards to keep in mind. As with photography, there may be subject-specific standards that you must adhere to; you supervisor will be able to point you in the direction of these if they are a feature of your subject. If there are no published standards, the following guidelines will help you to produce good-quality maps:

1. Consider using copyright-free maps and adding your own features instead of drawing or designing new maps. Google Maps allows you to save and annotate a map for use in an educational setting with proper attribution. For most uses of Google Maps, the attribution is included in the exported image.
2. Consider your experience with software and how much time you might have to learn how to use new software to create maps. For inexperienced users, I recommend Digimap (https://digimap.edina.ac.uk/), which most UK universities subscribe to, and Google Maps which doesn't require a subscription. For more experienced users or for more complex and customizable maps, take a look at QGIS (https://qgis.org/en/site/) which is open-source software with a variety of clear instructional videos to get you started.
3. All maps should include a scale and orientation reference. This is usually indicated in a corner of the map. You may need to rotate the north arrow on a map slightly, depending on your map view – don't automatically assume that north is up.
4. Make sure that the appropriate features that you want to draw your readers' attention to are clearly labelled and that a legend is included if necessary.
5. Use standard colours for your map features (if you choose to use colour). Colours which will make the most sense to your readers include using blue for water, green for vegetation, brown for open land, grey for roads, etc. Sticking to standardized colours makes your map accessible for your readers. Of course, the use of colour isn't essential and if you can effectively communicate the information you need in your map using back and white or greyscale, this means that your map will be completely colour accessible.
6. Don't include any redundant elements. As with academic writing, you should only include the essential information in your maps and other figures for clarity. For example, including political boundaries in a map designed to show the distance between two samples sites would be redundant and confusing.

Applying the evidence to your research

All of the different types of evidence discussed above can be used in your research to support your claims and arguments. Any claim that you make is only as strong as the evidence you present, so carefully consider the structure and content of your arguments. The recommendations below will help you to utilize scientific evidence to the best effect on your report.

1. Be informed by the evidence, don't look for evidence to fit your hypothesis.
2. Collect and evaluate the evidence before you incorporate it into your writing.
3. Only include relevant evidence in your writing.
4. Show how strong the evidence is through critical analysis.
5. Discuss any limitations and incorporate caution into your conclusions if necessary.
6. Combine evidence from several different sources to strengthen your argument.
7. Show why the evidence contributes to your claim/statement/ argument/finding.

Next steps

	If you are at the beginning of your research, start to think about the evidence you'll need to collect to answer your research questions
	If you have begun reading the literature and collecting data, write out your research questions and summarize the evidence you have collected to answer them so far. This will expose any gaps in your evidence that you can fill before your report deadline
	Think about the ethical implications of your project. Make a list of potential issues and discuss these with your supervisor
	Look up your institution's plagiarism policy

Writing a science dissertation

Introduction

Knowing what is correct and what isn't conventional in science writing is important if you are to write a good-quality dissertation. The information within this chapter is not just applicable to your dissertation – it applies to any and all science writing that you do. You'll notice that all professional science writing (published reports, books and journal articles) also follow these rules. This chapter explains the rules to follow when writing your dissertation, as well as showing you how to plan and structure each chapter or section of your report.

Topics in this chapter include:

- The fundamental characteristics of science writing
- How to recognize good and poor-quality science writing
- Structuring your dissertation.

Links between science writing and the scientific method

In the seventeenth century, at around the same time as the universal rules of science writing were being defined, The Royal Society developed and promoted the scientific method, credited originally to Francis Bacon. This 'new science' standardized the process of scientific investigation to remove bias and therefore increase the value and significance of discoveries that were made following the method. There is a close link between the scientific method and the principles of science writing, with clarity, objectivity and accuracy at the heart of both. Table 15 shows the various steps of the scientific method and their links with the core principles of science writing. Because the two practices (practical research and writing) are so strongly linked, your writing skills will directly contribute to your professional development as a scientist.

The steps of the scientific method	The link between the scientific method and science writing
Step 1: Observation	You will record many observations in your writing. These observations should be accurate and concise to make sure that they are understandable to your reader (the person marking your dissertation).
Step 2: Question	In science writing, questions must be focused to ensure that the work that follows has clear and constructive aims.
Step 3: Hypothesis	A written hypothesis, whether in a lab report, a dissertation or in an essay, needs to be clear and use accurate language. An experiment that tests the accuracy of equipment, for example, is different to one that tests the precision of the same equipment.
Step 4: Experiment	Even the most meticulous and considered lab experiment is of little use if it is not recorded clearly and concisely. The way an experiment is described determines how reproducible it is, which is important for its validity and credibility as scientific work.
Step 5: Analysis	Analysis in some form is ubiquitous in science writing and is an important feature of your dissertation. As soon as bias enters scientific work, it loses value.
Step 6: Conclusion	All conclusions in your work – during your dissertation and beyond – should be appropriately cautious. You may partially solve a problem, or you might confidently argue with supportive evidence, but always indicate how cautious or confident you are in your conclusions to give weight to them.

Table 15   How the scientific method can be linked to academic writing

The core principles of science writing

You may find that you intuitively follow some of these principles already and some you may be less familiar with. This section explains what the principles are and how to recognize your proficiency in each. If you know that you need to work on some of these rules, there is some guidance on how to improve each aspect in the context of your dissertation.

The rest of this section will examine each one of the core principles in turn, so that you can be confident that you are applying the rules to your own writing.

Principle	Definition
Clear	Writing should be comprehensible by all interested readers. You may need some background subject knowledge to understand the concepts, but the language should be plain and contain all the necessary detail required to understand the point.
Concise	You should be brief and to the point, whilst also fully conveying the message of the writing. Writing that includes lots of redundant words (often called waffle) is difficult for the reader to follow.
Unbiased	Above all, science is objective. Scientists work extremely hard to eliminate any bias from their research. This extends to science writing: everything you write should be backed up by independent facts and evidence, without the use of emotional language to persuade the reader.
Focused	Science writing should have a clear purpose which is indicated at the outset and stuck to in the rest of the work. Always try to stick to the point, without going off on a tangent.
Accurate	Every subject in science comes with its own nomenclature that is used in combination with standard vocabulary and units of measurement. Always using the correct language in writing will ensure that misinterpretations and mistakes are kept to a minimum.
Appropriately cautious	While you should make confident assertions about arguments that you have solid evidence for, you should equally show caution about arguments where the evidence is weak or scant.

Table 16   The core principles of science writing

Clear writing

A clearly written dissertation is easy to mark! Your theories, arguments, data and analyses are easy to identify, and contain all of the information in the correct order. Your marker doesn't need to look elsewhere in the text for context or supplementary data, because it's already included in your writing.

Example of unclear scientific writing

Evidence suggests that increased heat did not affect the health of rye (Secale cereale). There was no observable difference in plant height and maximum root length after 60 days. 50 plants were analysed in this category.

Example of clear scientific writing

Fifty rye (*Secale cereale*) plants were analysed to test the hypothesis that excessive heat has a negative effect on the health of this species: 25 plants were grown in an environment kept at 30°C and 25 plants were grown in an environment kept at an ideal growing temperature of 20°C. Plant height and root length were measured 60 days after seed germination as a marker of health. There was no difference between the measurements of plant height and root length in the two test groups, which suggests that excessive heat is not a factor in growing healthy rye.

Recognizing unclear writing

If you need to read a sentence or a paragraph more than once to understand the meaning of the writing, it is probably unclear. The example of unclear writing in the box on page 93 has information presented in the wrong order (logically, you would not discuss the evidence before you present it to your reader) and the reader could be easily confused into thinking that the length of the roots were being compared to the height of the plant because there is an incomplete comparison. Finally, some of the information needed to understand the point of the writing is missing: the reader needs to know how the fifty plants were tested to be able to understand the outcome. Reading your writing out loud can very often help you catch unclear writing as you are forced to process your work slower and more methodically than when you read in your head.

Improving unclear writing

Use this checklist to improve your unclear writing:

- Rewrite the information in the correct logical order.
- If you talk about data, refer the reader to a table or graph that contains that information.
- If you describe how something looks, refer to a picture or diagram that shows what you're describing.
- Check that you have included all of the necessary detail so that your reader doesn't have to look elsewhere in your writing or make assumptions about what you mean to say.

Concise writing

Concision is a simple case of quality over quantity. A ten-thousand-word dissertation that is written concisely will contain more information and will be of much higher quality than one of the same length that contains a lot of waffle.

Example of long-winded scientific writing

This shows a need to be clear about what exactly is meant by the phrase 'logical positivism' in this context. The term 'logical positivism' can also be referred to as being 'logical empiricism' and is the action of gathering and acquiring knowledge through the medium of direct observation, or through the application of logical proof.

Example of concise scientific writing

Logical positivism (also referred to as 'logical empiricism') is the acquisition of knowledge via observation or logical proof.

Recognizing long-winded writing

Excessively wordy writing takes a long time to explain a point. If your sentences are spanning several lines, or you are taking several sentences to explain a single point, you might want to look at how concise your writing is. Lengthy sentence introductions, such as the one seen in the example above, can also indicate that you are waffling. Additionally, if you find yourself writing a sentence and then rewording your point in the following sentence (recognizable by a sentence that begins with something like, 'that is to say') you're probably not being concise. Many writers use this method of rewording a point to increase clarity in their writing, but if you are able to write one, clear sentence instead of rewording a point, you're likely to end up with a clearer and more concise statement.

Improving long-winded writing

Use this checklist to improve your long-winded writing:

- Check that you haven't used a lengthy introduction to your sentence that doesn't add value to your writing.
- Look for groups of words that have the same meaning and delete one.
- Use the simplest form of a word, for example 'so' instead of 'consequentially'.
- If you are able to remove a word from a sentence and still retain the meaning of the sentence, that word is redundant and can be deleted.

Unbiased writing

The purpose of a science dissertation is to make observations and test hypotheses to increase our collective knowledge of your subject. It is important, then, that you base your findings on the evidence you collect.

Reporting your observations using an unfair or unrealistic interpretation of the data, or by including emotional persuasion, does not present an accurate description of your findings and leads to an incorrect understanding of your topic.

Recognizing biased writing

Writing that isn't appropriately objective often contains a lot of emotional language. If your writing focuses on persuading your reader using your choice of words, rather than using facts and evidence, you are likely to be presenting a biased point of view. Have a look at the tone you use when you write as well (see page 120 of this chapter). Biased writing can be quite casual and have a 'journalistic' tone that makes it sounds more like a newspaper article than a piece of academic writing. Being familiar with the tone used in academic journal articles will help you to strike the correct balance.

Example of biased writing

Thousands of majestic rhinoceroses have been brutally slaughtered in South Africa as a result of sheer ignorance. Poachers kill these beautiful animals because rhino horns are prized for their medicinal qualities in countries such as China and Vietnam. Tragically, this is a pointless exercise as we know rhino horn is made of keratin and has no proven health benefits. This dissertation will attempt to right these wrongs through the design and implementation of a programme of education that aims to set the record straight about the true value of rhinoceros horn.

Example of unbiased writing

An estimated 3,000 rhinoceroses have been killed in South Africa by poachers over the last three years (Gabriel, 2020). Poaching is driven by the high value placed on rhinoceros horn in countries such as China and Vietnam, where it is coveted as a symbol of social status and used in traditional Chinese medicine. The practical health benefits of rhino horn have been challenged repeatedly (Calk, 1983; Fenton, 1995; Biello, 2001; Driver, 2010); however, rhino populations continue to decline due to poaching. This dissertation attempts to address this issue through the design and implementation of a programme of education that aims to influence poachers to seek legitimate employment as rhinoceros conservators.

Improving biased writing

Use this checklist to improve your biased writing:

- Replace emotional statements with data.
- Avoid rhetorical questions and the use of exclamation marks.
- Use appropriate hedging language when talking about how convinced you are by the evidence.
- Focus on reporting the honest interpretation of your results and explaining why you got them, rather than trying to make your data fit your hypothesis.

Focused writing

Your dissertation should have a clear purpose which you indicate from the outset, and refer back to continually through the report. Writing that doesn't contribute to the overall purpose of your research (i.e. answering your research questions) simply cannot be awarded marks that contribute towards your grade, and is therefore wasted energy.

Example of unfocused writing

The 5th metatarsal is the most commonly broken bone in the foot. Bone is formed by two processes: endochondral ossification and intramembranous ossification. Endochondral ossification begins in the womb with the formation of a cartilage model, which is then gradually replaced by bone. Most of the bones in the body, including those of the toes, form in this way. Intramembranous ossification is the mechanism that forms flat bones like those of the skull. This process begins as a fibrous membrane where bone is deposited directly, without the initial cartilage model. A fracture of the 5th metatarsal might be treated with the use of an orthopaedic boot to immobilize the foot, or with a pressure bandage and weight bearing. Both of these treatments have been posited as the preferred treatment for a simple fracture, with no research, so far, that has directly compared the two methods in terms of cost and clinical outcome (Deakins 2015; Wheatley 2018). This research aims to fill this current gap in our knowledge via the systematic review of published medical literature.

Example of focused writing

The 5th metatarsal is the most commonly broken bone in the foot. A simple fracture might be treated with the use of an orthopaedic boot to immobilize the foot, or with a pressure bandage and weight bearing. Both of these treatments have been posited as the preferred treatment for a simple fracture, with no research, so far, that has directly compared the two methods in terms of cost and clinical outcome (Deakins, 2015; Wheatley, 2018). This research aims to fill this current gap in our knowledge via the systematic review of published medical literature.

Recognizing unfocused language

Writing that hasn't been initially planned can often become unfocused as you process the information you want to convey in your head, without organizing it first on paper. You may get halfway through a paragraph and then realize that you should have mentioned some background information to give context to the topic you're writing about (as in the previous example). This information then gets inserted into the middle of your paragraph and your writing goes off on a tangent. You might return to your original point, or you might continue your train of thought, but the result is the same: a section of writing that has little focus.

To identify this in your own writing, read each paragraph you have written and note the topic that it covers (either in the margin, or insert the topic in a line above each paragraph). Each paragraph should address one topic only, and the topics should be arranged in a logical order. For example, background information about a phenomenon should be presented before you go into any detailed description.

Improving unfocused writing

Use this checklist to improve your unfocused writing:

- Always plan each section using bullet points before you write.
- Address one topic per paragraph.
- Check that each paragraph logically follows the last.
- Isolate any new topics introduced in the middle of a section and either delete them if they are redundant, or move them to their own appropriate section in your writing.

Accurate writing

Science writing often features lots of technical terms and specialist language. It's important that this language is used correctly, and that all of the information required to understand your argument is included. A dissertation that includes lots of vague statements without the appropriate context will get a poor mark.

Example of inaccurate writing

The data interestingly shows, after a t-test was employed on each group to look at the differences in the means, that there is a high probability that proton beam therapy is better.

Example of accurate scientific writing

An independent t-test was performed on the patient outcome data (see table 2) and found a significant difference between the outcome of patients who underwent proton therapy and those who underwent chemotherapy. Equal variances were assumed, t (48) = 0.753 and P = 0.035. Patients who undertook proton therapy recovered on average 29 +/– 3 days faster than those who had chemotherapy. This suggests that proton therapy is more effective than chemotherapy in treating liver cancer.

Recognizing inaccurate scientific writing

To recognize inaccurate writing, re-read your work and think about how well it reflects the points you would like to make. If you use words (whether specific to your field or more general terms) without fully understanding their meaning, you run the risk of using them incorrectly. Similarly, if you're not fully confident about your topic, you will struggle to explain concepts and theories correctly. Identifying inaccurate writing therefore relies on your ability to recognize how well you understand the subject and the terms you use to discuss it: if you're not confident, it's possibly not accurate.

Improving inaccurate writing

Use this checklist to improve your inaccurate writing:

- Double-check your terminology. Common scientific terms that are often misused include 'accurate', 'precise', 'exponentially' and 'significant'. All of these terms can be found in the glossary of this book.

- Address incomplete comparisons. If you describe something as being greater or lesser (e.g. the largest specimen), make sure that you include both the thing that you're describing and the thing you're comparing it to (e.g. the largest specimen in the sample/population/world).
- Include all the detail required. Refer to tables/figures, and include all data for statistics (in an appendix if necessary).
- Explain the topic you're writing about out loud or, even better, to someone else. It's often easier to reword a statement to make it more accurate by speaking it than by writing it.

Appropriately cautious writing

Unfortunately, it is very rare to have definitive answers in any scientific field, and your dissertation should reflect this fact. Using language to indicate the strength of an argument or piece of evidence (yours or someone else's) will demonstrate a sophisticated understanding of your field and your research.

Example of inappropriately definitive writing

The results of this dissertation show that childhood obesity is predictable, and therefore preventable.

Example of appropriately cautious writing

Evidence presented in this dissertation suggests that it may be possible to predict the likelihood of a child being obese using parental BMI as an indicator. Children with parents in the normal BMI range were 2% likely to become obese by the age of 16, while children with obese parents were 67% likely to be obese by age 16. These findings, along with other well-established indicators such as activity levels and socioeconomic factors (Thamley 1992; Pritchard et al. 2000; Francis 2004), could be used to provide proactive support to children at risk of obesity.

Recognizing inappropriately definitive writing

Findings are rarely conclusive in science – there is almost always a limitation to the evidence presented. Overly definitive statements in science writing are often very short, very black and white, and provide little supporting evidence. Short, blanket statements about data or arguments should be reviewed to ensure they contain enough caution and supporting evidence.

Improving inappropriately definitive writing

Use this checklist to improve your definitive writing:

- Unless an entire population has been measured and the data are definitive, you must show caution in your writing when discussing results.
- Consider what other factors might be affecting measurements and think about what might explain variations in the data.
- You must then convey your caution in your choice of language: instead of stating that 'X proves Y', think about using 'X suggests Y', 'X is a likely indication of Y' or 'X is strongly linked to Y', depending on how sure you are of your statement.

Structuring your dissertation

The way in which you structure your dissertation will have a direct effect on how clear your dissertation is. A dissertation that lacks a well thought out structure is difficult to follow because information isn't presented in the order which your reader expects it to be, and may also be missing vital information that brings credibility to your work.

Spending a bit of time thinking about the structure of your dissertation will also make the job of writing such a long report much easier. By planning your structure, you break down the job into smaller, more manageable tasks that can be tackled one at a time. In this next section, we consider the structure of a typical science report. You should always double-check any guidelines about structure that are given by your institution as there may be small variations between different universities.

The beginning and the end

The first few pages of a science dissertation usually consist of the following.

Title page

Your title page should be simple and professional. Science dissertations rarely include images in their title pages. Your dissertation title should be the main feature of your title page, with your name and student number or identifier located somewhere underneath. There is usually also a statement of originality that confirms that the dissertation forms your own work – your institution will have guidelines about the specific wording of this, if it is required.

Check formatting rules related to your title page: you may need to use a particular font or to write your title in all caps. Although an incorrectly spelled or formatted title page is unlikely to lose you marks in itself, this is the first part of your work that your marker sees, so it pays to make a good impression (and to avoid putting them on the lookout for further mistakes).

Acknowledgements

Acknowledgements are included as a standard practice in academic publishing. They are not graded, but your marker will probably read them. This is your space to express gratitude to anyone who has helped you throughout your research. As a minimum, you may want to thank your supervisor and any staff that mentored you, as well as any funding bodies who supported you financially. It's important to keep your acknowledgements professional, but there's no reason you can't also thank your mum, granny, friend and/or dog. I've personally seen a PhD thesis that included a dedication to Polo mints, so feel free to express a bit of personality, while also remaining professional and appropriate.

Abstract

Your abstract is like the synopsis to your dissertation, so it makes most sense to write this last. Journal articles usually begin with an abstract, so you should be familiar with the kinds of details that are included in this short section of your dissertation. Your abstract should be around three hundred words and contain the following four aspects:

1. The purpose of your research.
2. The method/s you used.
3. Your main results.
4. Your headline conclusion.

Keep your abstract concise and focused. The example below contains all four elements of an abstract, without any redundant information.

A study of the physiological effects of pet therapy

Pet therapy, or animal-assisted therapy, has been gaining popularity in USA and UK medical settings since the 1980s. Patients and staff reported feeling calmed and reassured by interacting with dogs during pet therapy. However, the physiological benefits of this treatment are poorly understood. To explore this, we measured the heart rates of participants before, during and after a 10-minute interaction with a dog. All participants reported having no fear or anxious feelings towards dogs, and a control group was observed while viewing a photograph of a dog. The test group's heart rate measurements were lowest during their interaction with the live dog, while the heart rates of the control group did not vary significantly. We conclude that direct contact with dogs can produce positive physiological effects on the human body. Pet therapy can induce relaxation by slowing the heart rate, and could therefore be posed as an effective treatment for anxiety. Further research is proposed into whether the reported effects are long or short term.

Contents page and lists of figures, tables and equations

Creating your contents page and lists of figures and tables and equations should, like writing the abstract, be one of the last jobs you do in your dissertation. Ideally, you will write each chapter of your dissertation in a separate file and then put all of your chapters together to form one long dissertation document once your initial edits are complete (see the following section in this chapter and also Chapter 10 for more details on writing and editing your dissertation chapters).

Good lists of contents are clear and accurate. The easiest way to ensure this, if you are writing your dissertation in Microsoft Word, is to format each chapter title and section heading using the appropriate heading in the Styles gallery, located on the Home tab. To insert a table of contents, simply select Table of Contents from the References tab and choose an Automatic Table. This will give you a pre-formatted contents page which you should check to ensure that all chapters and sections have been included. To keep your contents page accurate, you should update the table of contents when you have finished editing your writing and before you hand in your dissertation by right-clicking the table and selecting Update Field.

A similar feature is available in Microsoft Word for figures, tables and equations (if you have these in your dissertation) by selecting Insert Table of Figures in the References tab. Select the appropriate caption label from the mini-toolbar (e.g. Figure, Table or Equation) and create a table for each list that you need. You should utilize the Insert Caption feature (also in the References tab) to create the captions for figures, tables and equations for this to work.

Of course, you could also create your lists manually, although this will take more time. However you choose to create your contents page and lists of figures, tables and equations, make sure that the formatting is consistent and that the lists are accurate.

Glossary of abbreviations and/or terms

Not every dissertation requires a glossary of terms or nomenclature, but if you choose to include one, place it after your contents lists and before your first chapter, which should be the Introduction. To decide whether you need to define abbreviations, specialist terms or technical nomenclature in your dissertation, consider how specialized the word or phrase that you'll be defining is and how often your use them in your dissertation. Commonly used terms in your field don't require an entry in a glossary. Terms that are not well known or that are unique to your research, however, should be defined. If you think that a list of definitions would help your reader to understand your research better, or would improve the flow of your writing, then it's probably a good idea to include one. Examples of appropriate entries in a glossary include organizational acronyms (e.g. SUERC – Scottish Universities Environmental Research Centre), units of measurement (e.g. eV – electron volt) and symbols (e.g. δ – delta).

Bibliography

The bibliography should be placed at the end of the last chapter in your dissertation. A bibliography must be complete, accurate and formatted in an appropriate referencing style (see chapter 9 for more information on referencing external sources and creating your bibliography). You might choose to use referencing software to build your bibliography, but you should always manually check the list yourself to make sure that all citations have been included and are correctly formatted.

Appendix

As with the glossary, not every dissertation requires an appendix. You will need to decide whether or not to include an appendix, but if you do, it should be placed right at the end of the dissertation. An appendix includes information that is part of your project, but that is not necessary to understand the meaning of your research. When deciding whether information should be included in the main body of the dissertation, or placed within an appendix, consider a) how important the information is and b) whether the inclusion of the information in the main body would interrupt the flow of your writing. For example, your marker will likely want to see evidence of working when you report the results of statistical tests in the discussion of your data. The inclusion of this information in the discussion chapter, however, would disrupt the focus and flow of the writing. In this case, it would be appropriate to report the results of the statistical test in the discussion chapter, and place the mathematical working in an appendix. Similarly, a blank questionnaire template would be a useful addition to a dissertation that includes survey data, however, to include this in the methods section of the report would not add much value to the chapter. Likewise, large amounts of raw data (either numerical data or qualitative data such as raw transcripts) are an important part of the research, but may require some processing to make the information meaningful. The raw data would be best placed in an appendix and the processed data would be reported in the results chapter.

The main body

Dissertations in science subjects usually follow a set structure, with each chapter having a specific purpose. Being aware of the purpose of each chapter will help you to understand what you will need to include in your writing and which of the fundamental principles of science writing to particularly focus on at any one time.

The next section will take you through each chapter of a dissertation and tell you its purpose, how to structure your writing to fulfil the expectations of the person marking your report and gives a checklist of essential elements to include at each stage.

1. Introduction

The first chapter of your dissertation, the introduction, gives your reader the background, context and a summary of your research. By the end of your introduction chapter, your reader should have a firm understanding of what you did in your research and why.

The purpose of the introduction is to 'set the scene'. This means that the chapter should be written using descriptive, rather than analytical, language.

A dissertation introduction, like the introduction to any piece of science writing, should be structured so that you move from the broadest background information to the finer details. This three-part structure (illustrated below) is the easiest for your reader to follow and makes the transition between the introduction and the literature review (your second chapter) seamless.

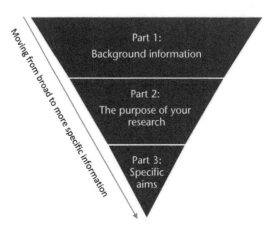

Figure 7   Illustrating the structure of an introduction

Part one of your introduction should identify the topic you'll be researching, and provide any background information that your reader might need to understand the later sections of your dissertation. Many students find getting the balance between providing too much detail and skipping over important issues difficult. Many more are unsure of the appropriate level of knowledge to pitch their writing and worry about being over simplistic with the detail they include. To overcome this, it is best to think about one of the main reasons you are writing the dissertation. While you are writing to make a contribution to your field and as a means of gaining experience in academic research, you are ultimately writing to be assessed: you will be submitting your dissertation for marking when you are finished. With this in mind, the appropriate level to write at is for an educated audience, with a background in your subject, but with no knowledge of the particular topic you are researching. Essentially, you should write for yourself, but at the beginning of the academic year. This should tell you something about both the level at which you should write, as well as the sort of detail you should include in the background to your topic.

With your topic identified, the introduction moves on to part two: describing the focus of your dissertation. To do this, tell the reader in a few sentences the issue/s you examined during the course of your research and why. Keep this description of your research brief. Don't, for example, begin to introduce the academic literature at this point because this will come in the next chapter, the literature review. In addition to telling your reader what you will be investigating, it's important to describe what you won't be considering. This is called defining the scope of your research, and its function is to show your audience the boundaries within which your dissertation lies.

Once you've summarized the research as a whole, you can then address even more focused information in part three: your research aims. In the final section of your introduction, it is helpful to list your research aims and objectives or your research questions. These don't have to be presented in paragraphs – in fact, lists such as these are usually clearer when presented in bullet points. Including a list of your aims and objectives or research question at this point will serve to focus your reader's attention on research as they begin to read the literature review. Finally, a good transition out of your introductory chapter is to summarize the structure of your dissertation. This means that your reader knows exactly what to expect from the rest of your report and, as a result, reading it will be far easier.

Note that aims are different to objectives: aims are the thing you want to do, and objectives are the ways you will do the thing.

Going back to the core principles of science writing discussed at the beginning of this chapter, clarity and focus are the most important rules to observe when writing the introduction. The introduction is often the first part of a dissertation that a marker will read, so a clear and well-structured chapter will stand you in good stead, while a poorly structured chapter with elements of irrelevant information will make it difficult to understand the rest of your work. Think about when in the writing process you'll write the introduction. Some students find that writing out the purpose and aims of the research helps to keep these important details at the forefront of their mind as they write later chapters. Others find it better to write the introduction towards the end of the writing process, when they are able to see exactly what their dissertation looks like on paper. Each approach has its advantages, and neither is right or wrong. In terms of word length, the introduction is one of the more brief chapters of your dissertation. The purpose of the introduction is to set the scene, not to construct arguments or introduce evaluation. For that reason, a good (rough!) guide to the right length for this first chapter is around 10 per cent of your total word count.

Essential elements checklist

A good-quality introduction:

- Gives the reader some background information on the topic of your research.
- Identifies the purpose of your research.
- Identifies your research aims/objectives/questions.
- Gives a brief summary of the structure of your dissertation.

2. Literature review

The literature review serves multiple purposes that all centre on justifying the value of your research. During the course of the review, you'll highlight and critique (both positively and negatively) published work to define the gap in current knowledge that you intend to fill or the problem that your research addresses. This, in turn, explains the thinking behind your research aims and questions. Reviewing the academic literature also shows the reader where your work sits in the complete body of knowledge, and validates your participation in the academic conversation. This justifies both your dissertation as a valid piece of research and you as a valid researcher.

From a less abstract point of view, the literature review serves to demonstrate many of the more complex research skills that your marker expects to see in your dissertation. After reading your review, your marker will have a firm understanding of the breadth and depth of the reading that you did for your dissertation. It also demonstrates how well you understood the papers you read and how well you identified the topics, issues and challenges associated with your research. Above all, the literature review should showcase your critical analysis skills, which are key to achieving a respectable grade for your work. So, the literature review is one of the most important chapters of your whole dissertation!

The three most important questions your literature should answer are:

1. Why is your topic worth considering?
2. What work has been completed already?
3. What are the possible outcomes of considering your question?

Before you begin writing the literature review, you must have completed the majority of your desk-based research and formulated the arguments you will convey in this chapter. See Chapter 6, Finding and analysing the literature, and Chapter 7, Using evidence in your dissertation, to find out more about conducting the research for your literature review. One of the more difficult decisions to make is to decide when a literature review is actually finished – especially if there is a wealth of literature available on your topic. The review is finished when you have entirely exhausted the range of topics and the papers relating to the key questions in your research. If you come across unfamiliar studies in the course of reading a journal paper, you're not done. Once you start to recognize citations and are familiar with all of the references that you come across, it's time to start writing that chapter!

Every literature review looks different: there is no one formula to follow and it is up to you as the researcher to decide what topics to include in the chapter. Not every paper or even every topic you read about in the research stage of your review will make it into the final chapter which might make up around 25–30 per cent of your total word count. When thinking about what will make up the content of your literature review, as well as how to structure this content, it helps to identify the most important topics that are related to your dissertation questions and aims: mind mapping can help in this endeavour.

When you have identified the main topics of your review, you'll need to decide the best logical order to address them. Look for the connections between your identified topics to find where one section might link nicely with another. Also think about what order you'll present this information in (see the example below for a template to follow). When deciding the order of your topics, think about the end goal of the review – to justify your research. Take your reader through each of the arguments in turn to show the questions that remain (that your dissertation will answer) or the gap in the knowledge (that you will address).

Example of a well-structured literature review:

Overarching dissertation question: How prepared are UK medical students to discuss illicit recreational drug use with their patients?

1. How big is the problem of drug-related deaths in the UK?
   - Drug-related deaths are at record high.
   - The rate of drug-related deaths is proportionally higher in the UK than it is in the EU.
   - Link to next section: Adequate clinical training is vital to address this significant problem.

2. What is the current training that medical students receive in relation in engaging patients in a discussion about recreational drug use?
   - Theoretical classroom training.
   - Practical training during placements.
   - Link to next section: How effective is this training?

3. What does the literature say about how prepared medical students feel to talk about recreational drug use with their patients?
   - Students are highly aware of the problem of substance misuse in the clinical setting.
   - Students report a lack of confidence in addressing the problem of drug use with their patients.
   - Most research has been conducted in England, so is not representative of the UK population.
   - Link to next section: We don't have currently enough data to answer the question sufficiently, and the data we do have suggests that medical students aren't prepared for conversations about drug use.

4. How does this dissertation overcome this problem?
   - Uses a multi-methodological approach to investigate the views of final-year medical students and investigate what changes to training/education are required to help prepare them for discussions with their patients about recreational drugs.
   - Adds data from students in Scotland to build a more representative picture of the issue in the UK.

Once you've identified an effective structure for your chapter, you can begin drafting out your sections. Returning back to the fundamental principles of science writing, the literature review is characterized by writing that is focused (which you have ensured via proper planning of the structure using a mind map), unbiased and appropriately cautious. You should aim to not just summarize or describe the literature, but to analyse it in the context of your research aims and questions. This means that for each one of your sections in the literature review, all of the claims that you make are backed up with evidence from the literature, but also that you weigh up the strength of that evidence (see Chapter 6 for more on creating a scientific argument). Make sure that your language remains formal and professional, and that you are attempting to convince your reader of your academic opinion using external evidence and not pleas to emotion. A good literature review is also fully up to date, so make sure that you check in with the prominent journals in your field even after you finish drafting your review to look for recently published papers that you should include in your dissertation.

A literature review as a research project

A literature review is an important section or chapter of a lab- or field-based report, but it can also be research in itself. Being able to synthesize and analyse a body of literature to give a new perspective on a topic or to come to a new conclusion about a collection of data or information is a valuable contribution to scientific knowledge. If you are conducting a literature review as standalone research, the structure of your report is the same as other forms of research. The difference is that your method chapter explains the databases and search strategies you used, and the 'data' is the information you collect from the literature. You can pool quantitative data from several articles and reanalyse it to come to a more confident conclusion about a research question. This is called meta-analysis, and is only valid if the data you use was collected using the same method or protocol.

Essential elements checklist

A good-quality literature review chapter:

- Covers all the topics relevant to your project.
- Includes all of the literature relevant to the topics.
- Critically analyses the literature (it doesn't just describe it!).
- Uses the literature to define the problem your research addresses or the gap in knowledge that you intend to fill.

3. Method

The method chapter is the recipe for the practical part of your research: it reports how your data was collected and treated to make it into something meaningful. Telling your reader the steps that you carried out to collect your data not only demonstrates that your data is accurate and reliable, but it gives the opportunity for others to use and adapt your method for their own research.

Your method chapter and the results chapter are the only predominantly descriptive chapters in your dissertation – everything else should have an element of critical analysis and evaluation included. Because you are reporting what you did in the data collection portion of your project, it makes sense to write your methods chapter at the beginning of the data collection process. This means that you are writing when the process is fresh in your head, but it also gives you a practical guide that you can use during data collection: you are far less likely to deviate or make small amendments to your method as you complete your practical work if you have already written the protocol down.

When detailing the materials you utilized in your research, there's no need to write in full paragraphs if a bullet point checklist would be clearer to the reader. Think about whether materials should be split into different categories, for example, a list of sites, a list of chemicals and a list of equipment might be a logical way of organizing a materials section.

After the list of materials should be a step-by-step description of the protocol you followed to obtain data. You may wish to present this as a numbered list for clarity – almost like a recipe. Write in full sentences and include enough detail so that the reader would be able to replicate your data collection procedure if they wanted to. If you followed a published protocol, you should direct the reader to the method via a citation before you describe the method.

As well as the steps you followed to collect the raw data, you should detail the process of organizing and analysing your data. This could include the application of computer modelling, statistical testing or normalization of data collected using analytical equipment. If you subjected your data to quality control tests, you should also describe these in your methods.

When reading your methods chapters, your marker will particularly focus on how clear and concise it is. It is the usually the shortest chapter of a dissertation and the easiest to write, since you are describing a process you should already be familiar with. If figures such as maps, schematics, photos or diagrams would aid the clarity of your methods, these should be added and referred to in the text.

Essential elements checklist

A good-quality methods chapter:

- Describes your approach to data collection.
- Describes how you will process the data once you have it.
- Includes enough detail for a peer to be able to replicate your work.
- Is written in plain, concise and descriptive language.

4. Results

The purpose of the results chapter is to report the raw data you collect. Many students confuse or incorrectly combine the results and the discussion chapters, but these should be separate sections of your dissertation. The results chapter contains the data and the discussion chapter tells the reader what the data means. The results chapter is descriptive and the discussion chapter is characterized by critical evaluation.

A good results chapter reports data clearly in tables (or the standard form for the data you have collected) and also summarizes the data in the chapter text. It helps to think about how you intend to report the raw data as you are collecting it so that you can format table headers and organize the data during your lab/field work. You should report ALL of the data you collect, even if you don't get the results you expect or if you know the data is of poor quality (because of a contaminated sample, for example). Highlight any data like this that you wish to exclude from the discussion chapter and describe your valid reason for exclusion in the summary of your results.

When writing about your results, remember that you should describe and summarize, without including any data interpretation. You may want to summarize the numerical range of the data, along with mean, median and mode values. It might also be appropriate to calculate the standard deviation or standard error of a group of data – this is perfectly acceptable, as long as you are not providing the reader with an interpretation of the data.

Example of effective data reporting:

Below is a summary table of all data collected during this research (table 4). All data that passed quality control indicators were employed to ensure that samples were not contaminated. All samples passed and were included in the discussion.

Sample no.	Sample origin	Temperature (°C)
15236	Skin	33.4
15237	Liver	36.9
15238	Brain	37.2

Table 4   Recorded temperature of research subject 1

The temperature measurements of subject 1 ranged from 33.4 to 37.2°C, with a mean value of 35.8°C ± 2.1°C.

Like the methods chapter, the results should be clear and concise. Accuracy is also fundamentally important to your results chapter. Don't ever be tempted to fabricate, amend or exclude data from your dissertation. The majority of research projects have some failures and unexpected data – you won't be penalized for this as long as you can explain the reason for your results in the discussion chapter that follows.

Essential elements checklist

A good-quality results chapter:

- Reports data without interpreting it.
- Includes the raw data in easy-to-read tables.
- Includes a full written description of the results.

5. Discussion

The discussion chapter should be, along with the literature review, one of the most substantial chapters of your dissertation (around 25–30 per cent of your word count). The discussion tells your reader what the data means and how it answers the research questions you identified in your introduction. The discussion also gives value to your research by placing it within the context of the published literature. By telling your reader where your dissertation sits in the current body of knowledge, you demonstrate your participation in the larger academic conversation in your subject.

Many students structure their discussion chapter by presenting the data according to the method of collection (e.g. survey data then interview data then focus group data). While this might seem like a logical way of presenting data, this structure can get messy when attempting to show how the data relates to the research questions. Instead, a much more effective way to structure your discussion is to identify your research questions and use the data to answer them in turn. This keeps the focus of your research on problem solving, rather than the mere production and interpretation of data. When addressing each research question, the following structure ensures you cover all the information your marker will look for.

1. Use your data to answer the research question.
2. Weigh up your evidence.
3. Place your findings in the context of the literature.

1. Using the data to answer your research questions
   When answering your research questions, use your data as the evidence to back up your claims. Think about how you present this data: if you have numerical data, what graph would best show the trend you are describing, and if you have qualitative data, think about what part/s of the data you will draw on to use as your evidence. When choosing your evidence, don't include any information that isn't relevant to the research question you are addressing: focus on showcasing one trend per data graph or making one point from an interview transcript.

   Question to consider:

   • How does the data answer your research questions?

2. Weighing up the evidence
   Once you have presented your evidence, you must then show how strong (or not!) it is. This shows how certain you can be that you have addressed the research question at hand, and also adds value and credibility to your findings. In numerical data handling, this strength may be exhibited via regression analysis of a perceived trend in a scatter graph or the use of standard deviation to indicate how precise the dataset is. For qualitative data, you might look at the frequency at which a topic was mentioned by participants, or you might analyse the type of language that was used when discussing certain subjects. For all types of data, consider what confounding factors might be involved in the relationship you are discussing. Are there any other factors that might explain the trend or pattern that you observed? Explain how confident you are of the true cause of the pattern. When discussing data, also consider what you can't tell from your research. For example, you may be able to prove that tryptophan has a calming effect on mice, but you may not be able to explain the mechanism behind the effect. It's important that you fully explore the meaning of your data so that your reader can see that your findings are well considered.

   Questions to consider:

   • How confident are you that the data answers your research question? Why?

- Are there any other explanations for your data?
- Could there be any other answers to your research questions that your data cannot address?

3. Placing your findings in the context of the academic literature
Considering your data in isolation is only the first step of your discussion. To really give weight to your findings, they must be placed within the context of the literature in your subject. This means comparing your findings to those in academic journal papers to show whether your research is backed up by a general consensus, in disagreement with the majority, an additional perspective on a topic or, indeed, poses new questions that are yet to be considered. All of these positions are perfectly acceptable – your research doesn't have to agree with the majority (as long as you have the evidence to back up your claims), but it's vital to show what your position is.

To establish the position of your research within the context of the wider literature, compare your findings with published literature as you answer your research questions. As well as providing direct comparisons between your findings and those of other academics, you should also provide a statement at the end of your data interpretation to summarize what your dissertation adds to the collective knowledge in your subject. You should have discussed the current state of knowledge in your literature review, so revisit this chapter of your dissertation to remind yourself of this and decide how your work contributes to your field. Adding this statement to your discussion chapter is also a really nice way of linking your literature review – where you shape your research questions, and the discussion – where you answer them. Refer your reader back to the literature review when discussing the collective knowledge.
Questions to consider:

- What do papers that asked similar questions using different methods find?
- What do studies that used similar methods but a different sample population find?
- What do the answers to the above questions say about the strength of your findings?
- If your findings are in contrast with those in the literature, what are the reasons for the differences and which position is more likely to be correct?
- What was the state of knowledge on your dissertation topic and how do your findings add to or change this?

Showing the limitations of your data

Discussing the limitations of your research is just as important as explaining to your reader what you can tell from your data. You should have identified the scope of your project in the introduction, so your reader has realistic expectations about your potential findings.

In the course of discussing your findings, however, it's common for the answers to predetermined research question to lead naturally to the development of further questions. In this instance, it's understandable that your data may not be able to answer these new questions, since your research wasn't designed with this new question in mind. While it's important to identify these new questions as it shows your reader you are able to think beyond the scope of your research, you shouldn't attempt to answer the question otherwise you risk stretching the meaning of the data further than is accurate and realistic. After all, this new research question could be the beginning of a whole new project!

As well as developing new research questions, you might find that you are only able to partially answer a question that you identified in the introduction of your dissertation. In this case, you should show both what the data does tell you and what it doesn't. Because your research was designed to answer the question in this case, you need to provide an explanation as to why the data wasn't sufficient. There should also be a suggestion of how the method could be amended to fully answer the question in future work. Similar to the approach to addressing data that didn't work, you won't be penalized for showing the limitations of your data in this way. It is a natural part of the research process, and you can demonstrate your understanding of this by highlighting these constraints. The example below shows how to address data that partially answers a predetermined research question.

> Samples were not available from all countries in the UK; data was not collected from individuals living in Wales as, despite extensive efforts, no people that matched the sample criteria could be identified. A larger canvassing campaign over a longer time period would possibly improve data collection from this region in future studies. Despite this, data collection from Scotland, England and Northern Ireland was very successful, and the low standard error values for data in these three regions indicate a representative sample was collected from each (see Table 6).

Discussing data that 'didn't work'

It is a normal part of academic research to get results that either don't match up with your hypothesis, or that are incorrect because of an error in the data collection process. Both of these scenarios are fine (although user error can be avoided through careful planning and execution of the experimental methods). If you knew that you were going to get perfect results at the outset of your research project, the value of the work could be seriously questioned, so don't worry about collecting strange and wonderful data.

The first step to dealing with erroneous data is to fully and accurately report it. Don't ever withhold or amend unexpected data to make the rest of your results look better quality. Once the data is reported in the results chapter, you can begin to address the causes in the discussion.

- Unexpected data: this is data that you know is accurate and precise, but doesn't conform to your hypothesis. In this instance, you should discuss the data in the same way as you would discuss data that did conform to your expectations. Address the data in the context of the appropriate research question, and offer the reader valid and unbiased reasons for the results that you observe. Discuss the data in the context of the literature, just as you would do with results that you did expect. With unexpected data, it is important to reaffirm the evidence for positing your null hypothesis at the beginning of your dissertation, alongside the reasonable explanation for accepting the alternative hypothesis at the end.
- Incorrect data: this is data that doesn't conform to your hypothesis because it is inaccurate. Perhaps equipment was malfunctioning, something wasn't set up right, a sample was contaminated or you simply made a mistake when collecting that particular bit of data. In this case, it is best to address this at the beginning of your discussion chapter. The aim is to explain the reason for the erroneous data, suggest a way this might be avoided in the future and then to indicate that you intend to disregard the data from further discussion. Because the data doesn't actually reflect a true observation, there is no value to using it to answer your research questions.
- Confusing data: this is data that doesn't conform to expectations, but the cause is unknown. It could be because it is unexpected or it could be incorrect, but there is no way of confidently deciding which of these is the case. In this case, discuss the data within the context of the research question, but acknowledge that your conclusions can only be very tentative because of the risk of the data being incorrect.

In all cases of data that didn't work, the best approach is honesty. Don't hide or manipulate the data – this goes against the fundamental principle of being unbiased in your research. If you can offer a reasonable explanation for your results, then this won't be judged negatively when your marker grades your dissertation. Indeed, negative results are still results that add to the body of knowledge in your subject.

Wrapping up your discussion

Once each of the research questions in your project had been identified and answered (or not!) using the data you have collected, you can wrap up the discussion chapter by revisiting the overarching aim of your research. Remind the reader of the one big reason for undertaking this project and summarize the importance of this reason once again. You can then go on to tell the reader whether your project was a success. The answer is most likely to be 'it was mostly successful', since it's rare for academic research to go 100 per cent as expected – and that is completely okay.

Essential elements checklist

A good-quality discussion chapter:

- Tells the reader what your data means.
- Uses the data to answer the research questions (these are your findings).
- Compares the data with findings in the academic literature.
- Identifies the strengths and limitations of your findings.

6. Conclusion

The conclusion brings all of your work together to form a headline statement that wraps up your research. This wrapping up process should have already begun at the end of the discussion chapter, which leads seamlessly into the conclusion to your dissertation. Because the purpose of the conclusion is to synthesize information, there should be no new ideas, data or literature introduced in this section of the report.

The structure of the conclusion should mirror that of the introduction in that it moves from very specific and focused information to the broader implications of the research (see Figure 8).

Begin by making a statement that summarizes the aims, method and key findings of your research. From this very specific point, you can then move to the wider implications of your work. The implications of your research are the answer to the big 'so what?' question in your dissertation. Why do your findings matter? What do they contribute? What do we know now that we didn't know before and how will that inform future research? Are there any practical applications of your findings that you can

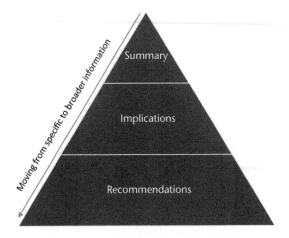

Figure 8   Illustrating the structure of a conclusion

demonstrate? Be careful not to simply repeat statements that you've made previously. Think further than just what your data shows, and instead consider why the research as a whole is important.

Returning to the fundamental principles of science writing at the beginning of this chapter, the conclusion should be appropriately cautious. It can be tempting at this stage of the dissertation to make statements that exaggerate or over-reach the true findings of the research. Good conclusions remain realistic about what the data shows, and can even reaffirm caution that should be exercised when interpreting the data you have.

Finish your conclusion by looking forwards to potential future research. Even if you never wish to think about your subject again, you should consider what might be next in the investigation of your topic. You might return to research questions that you developed in the discussion chapter and suggest some approaches to investigating these. Otherwise, you should consider what the next logical step would be now that you have added to the body of knowledge in your subject.

Essential elements checklist

A good quality conclusion:

- Sums up the answer to the research questions.
- Shows the potential effects of your findings.
- Provides recommendations for the practical application of findings for future avenues of research.

Fundamental writing rules

Knowing how to structure your dissertation and understanding the core elements of each chapter is only half of the job (unfortunately). As well as this, you will need to demonstrate a clear understanding of the mechanics of academic writing: this means maintaining appropriate tone, structuring paragraphs correctly and using punctuation accurately. This section will explain how to follow these fundamental writing rules.

Using the correct tone

The correct tone in science writing is always formal and professional. Think about the level of formality that you see in a journal paper – that's the tone you're aiming for. Formal science writing uses standard English, and the plainest and most direct words and phrases to convey information. The first thing to consider when selecting your tone is the universality of science writing. This means avoiding:

- Colloquialisms: these are commonly accepted words or phrases that are used, usually when speaking, rather than writing. They should be avoided because these are rarely understood outside the geographical region they are used. For example, someone outside the north of England might not understand what the word 'mithering' means, so it doesn't make sense to use the term in writing intended for a global audience.
- Slang: this is more informal than a colloquialism and may only be used by certain groups of people (e.g. teenagers) rather than being used by everyone in a particular region. Avoid slang because these terms may not be understood outside the group of people that commonly use them.
- Abbreviations: abbreviating words using an apostrophe, such as 'don't', 'can't' and 'shouldn't', should be avoided as the clearest way to write these terms is fully, e.g. 'Do not', 'cannot' and 'should not'.

The second aspect to consider when thinking about correct tone is to consider the professionalism of science writing. Science should always be reported objectively, so we should avoid attempting to convince our readers with emotive language. As scientists, we should convince using external evidence only. This means avoiding:

- Exclamation marks: these should be avoided as they are too informal and the meaning is often open to reader interpretation. Formal and clear science writing always aims to persuade using words, rather than punctuation.
- Rhetorical questions: these are questions that you pose to the reader without providing an answer. Like exclamation marks, rhetorical

questions inhibit the clarity of science writing as they are open to interpretation. Also, especially in an assessed piece of work, the writer is required to provide answers to all of the questions they pose to demonstrate their understanding of the topic.

- Pleas to the readers' emotions: using anything other than external evidence (e.g. data, models, published theories, etc.) is not acceptable as it introduces bias into your writing. If you are unable to provide evidence for a claim, you cannot reasonably make it.
- Journalistic language: this is a distinct style of writing found in publications aimed at the wider public – e.g. blogs, newspapers, magazines. Journalistic writing has the potential to be objective; however, the primary reason for journalistic writing is to inform in an interesting way that is accessible to the widest audience. Science writing, on the other hand, favours accuracy over interest, and the audience is much narrower so language and terms are much more specific.

Hitting the correct tone in science writing becomes easier with practice. While you are honing your tone, it can help to read journal articles in your field (which you'll be doing anyway as part of your research). Notice the formality of the language and the ways in which the writers persuade their readers, then try to emulate that in your own writing.

Planning a chapter and structuring a paragraph

Paragraph structure basics

- Address one topic per paragraph.
- Put your topics in a logical order.
- Link your paragraphs with transitions.
- Use the structure: claim → reason → evidence → conclusion.

A dissertation or project report is full of complex information and scientific argument. Properly structured paragraphs help to make that complex writing easier to understand. To end up with well-structured paragraphs, it's best to begin by thinking about the overall structure of the section you want to write and then consider how you'll put the individual paragraphs together. Hereare some guidelines to help you build an effective writing plan for a report section or dissertation chapter:

1. Each paragraph should address one topic, claim or point. If you find yourself including two or more topics in the same paragraph, it will need splitting up into several separate paragraphs. Addressing one topic at a time means that you can fully and effectively unpack the

background information required to understand the topic, as well as the evidence needed to support any claims. Paragraphs that address more than one topic often lack the depth of detail or evidence required to form a complete argument. Writing about more than one topic at a time also requires your reader to retain multiple points in their mind as they process the information, making the writing difficult to follow.

2. Paragraphs should be logically ordered when planning your writing, so first think about the topics you need to write about, and then think about the order in which you'll address them. Add these topics to a word document and bullet point them – these are the headings you'll use to plan your writing (have a look at the example on page 109 about structuring a literature review to see how to decide the order of paragraphs).

3. One you have planned the topics you'll write about, you need to think about how to link the various headings together. Linguistic transitions show the relationship between two paragraphs. Some topics don't need explicitly linking with a transition because they are so closely related. Indeed, writing that contains transitions between every paragraph can lack quality of content and seem overly wordy. Where you are moving to a different topic, for example when introducing a counter-argument to a claim you've been discussing, a transition sentence or paragraph is needed so that the sudden change in topic doesn't seem jarring. Don't worry about how to word the transitions at this stage, just make a note of where they are required in the bullet-point plan.

4. Once you have a solid plan for the chapter or section you want to write, you can begin writing! To properly structure a paragraph, make your statements in the following order:

   1. Claim or topic introduction: this is a sentence that lets the reader know exactly what you'll be arguing for/against, or the topic you'll be discussing.

   2. Reason or context: after making your introductory statement, you either want to state the reason for believing the claim or to provide some broader background information on the topic.

   3. Evidence or examples: back up your argument with reliable external evidence (data, statistics, findings from the literature, etc.) or provide examples to clarify the topic for the reader. This part of the paragraph could span several sentences as you unpack evidence from multiple sources.

4. Conclusion and (if required) transition: sum up the main findings from your argument and wrap up the topic. If you've identified in the planning stage that a transition statement is required, put that right at the end of your paragraph

Exercise 4: Structuring a paragraph

The example paragraph below contains all of the elements of a well-structured paragraph. Test yourself by identifying each of the elements. The answers can be found at the end of this chapter.

We found that modern marine samples are suitable for inclusion in ancient faunal isotope baselines. Extensive isotope data showed that modern marine bone and ancient marine bone are comparable in both carbon and nitrogen values. A t-test was carried out to compare the modern isotope values to the ancient measurements. No significant statistical difference was found between the two datasets ($p>0.05$). This finding correlates with previous studies carried out on samples from South Africa (Smith et al. 2010), and Iceland (Murdoch 2015). These studies used isotope analysis on good-quality datasets (>100 samples for each species) and found no significant difference between ancient and modern fauna. These findings strengthen the findings of the data in this dissertation, and also the hypothesis that modern marine samples can be used to supplement ancient faunal isotope baselines.

Next steps

	Think about which of the fundamental principles of science writing that you currently excel at, and those that will need a bit of practice to hone
	Plan the structure of your dissertation. Decide on your chapter headings and draft the subheadings that you will include in each chapter

Exercise 4: Answers

1. Claim: We found that modern marine samples are suitable for inclusion in ancient faunal isotope baselines.

2. Reason: Extensive isotope data showed that modern marine bone and ancient marine bone are comparable in both carbon and nitrogen values.
3. Evidence: A t-test was carried out to compare the modern isotope values to the ancient measurements. No significant statistical difference was found between the two datasets ($p>0.05$). This finding correlates with previous studies carried out on samples from South Africa (Smith et al. 2010), and Iceland (Murdoch 2015). These studies used isotope analysis on good-quality datasets (>100 samples for each species) and found no significant difference between ancient and modern fauna.
4. Conclusion: These findings strengthen the findings of the data in this dissertation, and also the hypothesis that modern marine samples can be used to supplement ancient faunal isotope baselines.

Avoiding plagiarism in your research

Introduction

The topic of plagiarism can often seem quite intimidating if you haven't already spent a little time finding out about what it is and how to avoid it. Although plagiarism is taken seriously at university, avoiding it is usually as simple as being aware of the rules and understanding how to reference sources correctly. The basic principle is that all work you complete during your studies is your own and where you have used someone else's work in your research, the original author is acknowledged. Plagiarism is closely connected to academic integrity – by not plagiarizing, you know you will receive the correct and fair grade for your work.

Topics discussed in this chapter:

- Defining the different types of plagiarism
- How plagiarism is detected and managed
- Avoiding accidental plagiarism
- Referencing correctly
- Some advice on keeping track of your references.

What is plagiarism?

In short, plagiarism is including someone else's work in your own submissions, without properly acknowledging the source, or including any element of work that has, in part or in whole, been submitted in another assessment. Of course, there's more to it than that, but plagiarism really is just passing someone else's work off as your own. Each higher education institution has an academic integrity policy that states how they maintain high academic standards of honesty and transparency to ensure that your degree is valuable and credible – I strongly recommend that you look up the policy for your institution (it should be freely accessible on their website). It is especially important for you to understand the rules of academic integrity if you are studying in a different country to your home country because there can be differences in what is acceptable. Below, we discuss different types of plagiarism that you are likely to see described in an academic integrity policy. Knowing about these will help you to avoid them.

Collusion

If you work with other people on individual assignments, this is called collusion. Collusion gives you the unfair advantage of an extra brain and pair of eyes, which is why it is considered plagiarism. There may be times in your degree where you are required to work in a group, and in these circumstances, you should be able to demonstrate your own individual contribution to the work to demonstrate that you have not plagiarized. Your research project is more than likely an individual assignment. While it is perfectly acceptable to work with your fellow students in reading or writing groups where you are all working on your individual projects in the same virtual or physical space, it is not appropriate for anybody within (or outside) those groups to contribute to the content of your work: they can't make your data graphs or write a portion of your literature review, for example.

Accidental plagiarism

Plagiarism is treated with very similar consequences whether you intended the infringement or not. This means that if you forget to credit an original source, if your paraphrased version of a source is too close to the original or if you don't properly indicate which part of your writing is yours and which you have quoted from elsewhere, you have plagiarized. Most students don't set out to cheat, so accidental plagiarism is the most common form of plagiarism seen in assessment submissions. The way to avoid this type of plagiarism is to have a clear understanding of how and when to reference external sources. This is addressed in the second part of this chapter.

Auto-plagiarism

Auto-plagiarism, or self-plagiarism, is committed if you hand in all or part of a piece of work for multiple assessments. This means that if, for example, you wrote a critical review for a course that is related to your research topic, you cannot copy and paste any element of that review to use in your project report. Auto-plagiarism is considered a poor academic practice because submitting the same piece of work for multiple assessment does not properly demonstrate what you have learned in each individual course (which is the purpose of assessment).

Plagiarism in non-written work

Most cases of plagiarism are committed in written work, but all the rules of academic integrity apply to exams, presentations and video/audio assessments as well. You may be asked, for example, to give a slideshow presentation that outlines your research proposal as part of your project assessment. All the standard rules of working on individual work and crediting external sources applies to the slides you present and the talk that you give.

How is plagiarism detected?

Plagiarism is detected by markers in a number of ways. There is a wide range of plagiarism detection software that searches for similarities between a database of known papers and the paper submitted by the student. This type of software, while sophisticated and extremely accurate, is only an initial safety net used to detect plagiarism. The vast majority of instances of plagiarism are detected by the person marking an assessment. Lecturers are adept at spotting elements of writing that look amiss, and they are aware of certain indicators of plagiarism that will prompt them to investigate further. This twin approach to plagiarism detection means that it is never worth attempting to sneak anything past the professionals. The gains are very little and the potential consequences are severe.

What are the penalties for plagiarizing?

If you are accused of plagiarism your university will have a defined protocol that they will follow to investigate the accusation and decide an adequate outcome if you are found to have broken the rules of academic integrity. The processes may differ slightly between different institutions, but generally speaking, you will be given a chance to hear why you have been accused of plagiarism and also an opportunity to explain yourself to a panel. You should be allowed to take someone with you to this meeting to either formally represent you (e.g. someone from your student union) or simply to provide informal support (e.g. a friend).

The potential outcome will probably depend on a number of factors, including the type and severity of the plagiarism (e.g. paraphrasing an article without providing a citation vs. copying and pasting elements of other people's work to make your essay), whether the plagiarism was accidental or not, how many times you have previously committed plagiarism and what level of study you are currently in (the penalties for final-year undergraduates or postgraduate taught-students are far heavier than those for level 1 or 2 undergraduates). The full circumstances of the plagiarism will be considered, and possible outcomes include:

- A formal, recorded warning.
- Taking part in mandatory plagiarism training.
- Resubmitting your work (without the plagiarized elements).
- Resubmission and grade cap applied (i.e. you will only be able to earn a D grade, even for a piece of work that would ordinarily have achieved an A).
- A reduction in the grade or a mark of zero for the assessment.
- Failure to pass the module in which the plagiarized assessment was submitted.
- Reduction of degree classification (e.g. a 2:1 would be reduced to a 2:2).
- Expulsion from the institution.

Avoiding accidental plagiarism

Accidental plagiarism can be avoided by knowing the rules around academic integrity at your institution and by proper planning of your work and your time. The latter is particularly important for longer research reports and dissertations because there will be a considerable amount of sources to cite and manage. As part of my job, I speak to students who have plagiarized in their work. We discuss what happened and how to avoid plagiarism in the future. The vast majority of these students never intended to break the rules and there are clear patterns in the reasons for making the mistakes that they do. Based on those patterns, here's some guidance for avoiding accidental plagiarism:

Give yourself enough time

A typical scenario for students who accidentally plagiarize is that they realize they have only a couple of days until their deadline with very little writing done. In a panic, they begin copying and pasting the odd sentence from external sources instead of taking the time to think about how a source should be paraphrased. If you find yourself in the unfortunate situation of having run out of time, far better to hand in a shorter report that has been well considered than to try to 'bulk out' the word count with phrases from the literature.

Be clear in your note-taking

When making notes from papers that you are reading, be in the habit of summarizing points in your own words and be very clear when you use direct quotes in your notes. This means that if you copy parts of your notes verbatim, you won't accidentally copy the original source. Also note down the author, date and brief title for each source you use.

Referencing sources properly

The best way to avoid committing plagiarism is to know how to reference. You will be required to mark each reference to an external source with a citation in the text, and then give the full source details as a reference in the bibliography. There are lots of different referencing styles (or systems), and the way you format a reference is dictated by the type of source you're referring to. While that might seem complicated, you don't have to know how to do all of that off by heart. All you need to know is what to cite and how to use a reference system guide.

Why do we reference?

As you write your dissertation, you will need to refer to numerous external sources to back up your claims, strengthen your findings and supplement your data. Using external reference from the academic literature links your research with the current knowledge in your field, so you can show how your work contributes to this body of knowledge. If you don't cite (or only cite minimally) in your dissertation, your work won't have the same value and credibility as a report that has its research questions linked to gaps in understanding and its results discussed in relation to studies that have investigated similar research questions. For more information on how to incorporate evidence from the academic literature into your work using direct quotations and paraphrasing, see Chapter 7 in this book.

What do I cite?

The rule on what information requires a citation is quite simple: if the statement does not belong to you and it isn't common knowledge in your field (anything that isn't debated can be accepted as common knowledge), then it requires a citation.

Any of the following that **you didn't produce** should be cited:

- Data
- Theories
- Arguments
- Models
- Figures and diagrams
- Conclusions
- Interpretations
- Direct quotes (written or spoken)
- Practical method
- Computer code, programs and algorithms.

You can incorporate external evidence into your writing by either paraphrasing the original or providing a direct quotation.

Paraphrasing

Paraphrasing is explaining an element of an original source in your own words. The vast majority of the sources you cite in your research should be paraphrased, rather than directly quoted. A paraphrase demonstrates that you have a deep understanding of the original material and that you can apply the concepts to back up a scientific argument. A direct quote, on the other hand, doesn't demonstrate this understanding as much, and only shows that you know where the phrase you used would fit in the context of your writing.

To appropriately paraphrase a piece of writing, you must avoid simply rewording the original. Similar to a direct quote, rewording the original doesn't adequately demonstrate your understanding of the work you are referring to. Also be wary of close paraphrasing, which is where the wording of a paraphrased piece of text is too similar to the original. To properly paraphrase a source, think about the following:

- Why are you using that particular piece of evidence?
  We use references in academic work to support our claims or arguments. Think about the link between your claim and the source you want to refer to and identify how the source supports the claim.

- What part of the original do you need?
  Very often, a close paraphrase occurs because a writer rephrases an entire sentence or paragraph, without considering what part of the original is needed to support their claim. You may only need to use a small element of the source because the rest is irrelevant to your argument.

- Put the original out of sight when you write about it.
  Referring to a source as you paraphrase it is more likely to result in a close paraphrase as you focus on the wording of the original instead of

the idea and the link between that and your claim. Instead, read the original and once you have decided on the link with your work and the element of the evidence that you need, put the original away before you write about it.

- Go back and check the source.
  When you have finished paraphrasing, re-read the original to make sure that you have understood and accurately represented the source without repeating any of the phrasing.

Exercise 5: Paraphrasing

Below you will see an extract from a real journal article. There are two paraphrased examples that follow. One example is of a paraphrase that is too close to the original and would be considered plagiarism. The other is an acceptable way of paraphrasing the original. Read the original statement and both examples and decide which example is acceptable and which is not. The answers are at the end of this chapter.

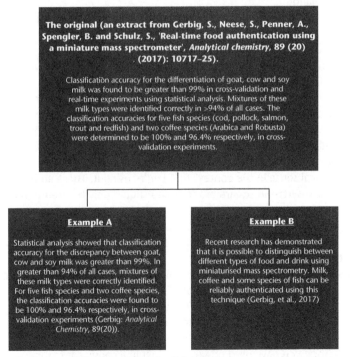

The original (an extract from Gerbig, S., Neese, S., Penner, A., Spengler, B. and Schulz, S., 'Real-time food authentication using a miniature mass spectrometer', *Analytical chemistry*, 89 (20) (2017): 10717–25).

Classification accuracy for the differentiation of goat, cow and soy milk was found to be greater than 99% in cross-validation and real-time experiments using statistical analysis. Mixtures of these milk types were identified correctly in >94% of all cases. The classification accuracies for five fish species (cod, pollock, salmon, trout and redfish) and two coffee species (Arabica and Robusta) were determined to be 100% and 96.4% respectively, in cross-validation experiments.

Example A

Statistical analysis showed that classification accuracy for the discrepancy between goat, cow and soy milk was greater than 99%. In greater than 94% of all cases, mixtures of these milk types were correctly identified. For five fish species and two coffee species, the classification accuracies were found to be 100% and 96.4% respectively, in cross-validation experiments (Gerbig: *Analytical Chemistry*, 89(20)).

Example B

Recent research has demonstrated that it is possible to distinguish between different types of food and drink using miniaturised mass spectrometry. Milk, coffee and some species of fish can be reliably authenticated using this technique (Gerbig, et al., 2017)

Figure 9 An excerpt from a published article with two paraphrasing options. (Gerbig, S., Neese, S., Penner, A., Spengler, B. and Schulz, S., 'Real-time food authentication using a miniature mass spectrometer', *Analytical chemistry*, 89 (20) (2017): 10717–25)

Questions to consider:

1. Which of the examples would be considered plagiarism, and why?
2. Which of the examples do you think demonstrates the best understanding of the original, and why?
3. Which of the citations is correct?
4. Why didn't Example B use the numerical data given in the original?

Direct quotes

Direct quotes use the original wording of a source as evidence in your writing. It is essentially copying and pasting a phrase, sentence or (rarely) a paragraph. A direct quote isn't as commonly used in STEM subjects as it is in the arts: this is because arts subjects often use logical argument as the evidence for their knowledge, and therefore, retaining the wording of an original source is important to represent it accurately. The sciences, on the other hand, are far more likely to use data and statistics as the evidence for their knowledge and it doesn't matter how you word these, the meaning will not change.

In science, you should only directly quote a source if the original wording is important, and paraphrasing it has the potential to inaccurately represent the source. For example, laws and legal statements, and the rules or guidelines of governing bodies are always worded in carefully considered ways and paraphrasing these might not accurately represent the original when you refer to them in your writing. Keep quotes as brief as possible, and only quote the vital information. You may want to use ellipses (…) to indicate that some irrelevant information was removed from the original, and you might also want to insert a word such as 'and' or 'but' to ensure the quote makes grammatical sense in the context that you're using it. These additions should be inserted in square brackets and should only be used to make the sentence clearer.

When directly quoting an original source, you must separate the original from your own words by enclosing it in quotation marks. Quotation marks may be double (") or single ('), and the referencing system that you use in your writing will usually define which type to use (for example, APA asks for double quotation marks). Where the type of quotation marks are not specified, use single quotation marks to quote text, and double quotation marks to quote speech. Even if you get the single/double decision wrong, you won't be penalized or accused of plagiarism if you have used one or the other in a consistent manner throughout your writing. Note that it is perfectly acceptable to use someone else's unaltered data in your work and this doesn't need quotation marks (though it does need a citation and a reference). Mathematical theorems also don't need quotation marks.

Restrict the length of direct quotes to only as long as absolutely necessary. A quote that is longer than a couple of lines should be set in your writing as a separate indented paragraph. In every case, a citation for a quote should be placed immediately after the closing quotation marks and not at the end of the sentence that contains the quote.

Exercise 6: Direct quotes

Below is an extract from an original document that you might cite in your research. The statement can be found in the International Health Regulations published by the World Health Organisation (WHO). Read the original text and the two examples and decide which one is correct.

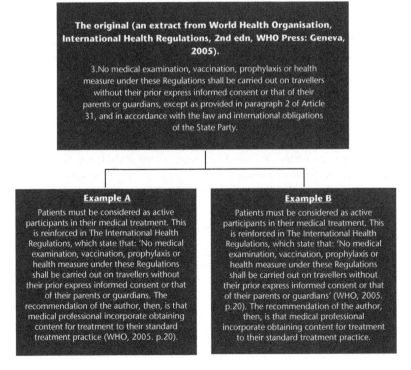

Figure 10   An excerpt from World Health Organisation regulations with two direct quotation options. (World Health Organisation, International Health Regulations, 2nd edn, WHO Press: Geneva, 2005.)

Questions to consider:

1. Which of the examples would be considered plagiarism, and why?
2. Why would the original be quoted instead of paraphrased?
3. Would it be appropriate in either example to use ellipses to remove some words or phrases?

How do I cite?

There are several systems that are used to cite and reference external sources in academic writing. The system you use might be prescribed to you by subject conventions (e.g. Psychology papers nearly always cite using the APA style), but more commonly you will simply be required to select a style to use in your dissertation. It's worthwhile checking your individual institution's dissertation requirements to check whether you should be using a particular system. There are far more systems than are detailed in this book, but a guide to producing correct references and citations in two of the most commonly used styles can be found below. Note that there are different formats for different types of source (e.g. website vs. journal article) so if you need to cite something that isn't on the list (e.g. conference proceedings or a newspaper article) you'll need to check the style guide for each system, which can usually be found for free online or through your institution's library.

Author-date style

In-text citations

Citations can be written in one of two ways: either place the citation at the end of the sentence containing the source (parenthetical citation) or incorporate the citation into the sentence itself (narrative citation).

- When citing one author
  Parenthetical citation: Research shows that backing up a statement with a valid reference strengthens an academic argument (Bank 2021).

  Narrative citation: Research by Bank (2021) has shown that backing up a statement with a valid reference strengthens an academic argument.

- When citing two or three authors
  Parenthetical citation: Research shows that backing up a statement with a valid reference strengthens an academic argument (Bank and Turner 2021).

  Narrative citation: Research by Bank, Turner and Finley (2021) has shown that backing up a statement with a valid reference strengthens an academic argument.

- When citing four or more authors
  Parenthetical citation: Research shows that backing up a statement wIth a valid reference strengthens an academic argument (Bank et al. 2021).

  Narrative citation: Research by Bank et al. (2021) has shown that backing up a statement with a valid reference strengthens an academic argument.

References

Each citation should have an associated reference in the bibliography, which is arranged alphabetically according to the first author's surname.

- Journal article
  Author surname, Initials., Year. Title of Article. *Journal name,* Volume(issue), pp. Page range.

  Example: Bank, I.M., Turner, J.V. and Finley, M.M., 2021. Investigating the persuasiveness of evidence-based academic writing. *Journal of Academic Writing,* 8(5), pp. 235–279.

- Book
  Author surname, Initials., Year. *Title of Book.* Edition (if not the first edition). City or town of publication: Publisher.

  Example: Bank, I.M., 2021. *The Persuasiveness of Academic Writing.* Oxford: Hopewell Press.

- Book chapter
  Chapter author surname, Initials., Year. Title of chapter. In: Book editor surname, Initials., ed./eds. Year of book, *Title of book.* Place of publication: Publisher. pp. Page range.

  Example: Bank, I.M., 2021. Academic writing and critical analysis. In: Turner, J.V. and Finley, M.M., editors. 2021, *The Fundamentals of Academic Writing.* Oxford: Hopewell Press. pp. 19–64.

- Website
  Author or organization, Year. Title of webpage or document [online]. Available at: URL [Accessed dd/mm/yyyy].

  Example: Bank, I.M., 2021. Guide to Harvard referencing at the University of Hopewell [online]. Available at: https://www.hopewell.ac.uk/academicguides/harvardreferencing [Accessed 30/04/2021].

Numeric system

In-text citations

In a numeric system, citations are given as numeric labels which are placed after the source in your writing. You can refer to the author within the sentence, in a similar way to a narrative citation in the author-date style, but you must also place a numerical label along with the author's name.

- Citing without reference to the author/s
Research shows that backing up a statement with a valid reference strengthens an academic argument.[4]

- Citing with reference to the author/s
One author: Research by Bank[9] has shown that backing up a statement with a valid reference strengthens an academic argument.

  More than one author: Research by Bank et al.[9] has shown that backing up a statement with a valid reference strengthens an academic argument.

References

Each citation should have an associated reference in the bibliography, which is arranged numerically according to the order that they appear in the text.

- Journal article
Author surname, Initials. Title of article. *Journal name.* Year; volume(issue): page range.

  Example: Bank I.M., Turner J.V. and Finlay M.M. Investigating the persuasiveness of evidence-based academic writing. *Journal of Academic Writing.* 2021; 8(5): 235–279.

- Book
Author surname, Initials. *Title of Book.* Edition (if not the first edition). City or town of publication: Publisher; Year.

  Example: Bank, I.M. *The Persuasiveness of Academic Writing.* Oxford: Hopewell Press; 2021.

- Book chapter
Chapter author surname, Initials. Title of chapter. In: Book editor surname, Initials, editors. *Title of book.* Edition (if not the first edition). City or town of publication: Publisher; Year. Pp. Page range.

  Example: Bank, I.M. Academic writing and critical analysis. In: Turner, J.V. and Finley, M.M., editors. *The Fundamentals of Academic Writing.* 2nd ed. Oxford: Hopewell Press; 2021. Pp. 19–64.

- Website
Author or organization. Title of webpage or document [Internet]. Town or city of publication: Publisher; [updated year month date; cited year month date]. Available at: URL [Accessed dd/mm/yyyy].

  Example: Bank, I.M. Guide to Harvard referencing at the University of Hopewell [Internet]. Hopewell: University of Hopewell; [updated 2018 June 18; cited 2021 April 30]. Available at: https://www.hopewell.ac.uk/academicguides/harvardreferencing [Accessed 30/04/2021].

Know how to proofread and edit your own work

Proofreading and editing is an academic skill that is part of scientific research. For this reason, it's usually expected that you will check and edit your own work, including checking your citations and references. In certain situations (e.g. you are not writing in your native language, or you have a disability that requires extra learning support) external proofreading is okay, but this should be a service that is approved by your institution. Never pay an external commercial company or person for proofreading services without speaking to your institution first or you might unwittingly plagiarize (and waste your money in the process).

How do I keep track of my references?

Dissertation research usually comes with a long list of references that must be properly formatted and organized. Bibliographies will often span several pages in length, so it makes sense to think about how you will manage all of this information to make sure that nothing gets omitted or incorrectly formatted. There are a host of software programmes that are designed to help you store, organize and manage your citations and references. Below are the programmes that I recommend (table 17). Most of the programmes are free (or at least have a workable free version), but universities often provide referencing software free to their students. Check with your library or IT department to see what they provide.

Conclusion

Academic integrity is taken quite seriously in UK Higher Education for a couple of reasons. First, if all students submit their own work and acknowledge when they have incorporated external sources into their assessment, everyone gets a fair mark. A wider reason for having such clear rules is rooted within academia and the way we grow and develop our knowledge. Scientific progress only advances if research is shared so that it can be reviewed and amended or built upon. This open sharing of knowledge is underpinned by the understanding that the work can be used by other researchers (such as yourself) but must be credited to the original person. Without these universally agreed-upon rules about academic integrity, that sharing of knowledge becomes far less open and free. So next time you're citing a journal paper, remember that you're contributing to scientific progress!

Software	Cost	Pros	Cons
Microsoft Word Citations and Bibliography tool	Free (included with the cost of Microsoft Word).	Easy to use with no additional software to install. The tool can be found in the 'References' menu on the Microsoft Word main toolbar.	No facility to import references from the web. No option to store or organize papers. All information has to be manually typed into the toolbar fields, which can take time when dealing with a lot of different sources.
Zotero	Free for limited storage, with further paid premium options available.	Zotero is open source. It can be used online or locally and can import and annotate citations from a range of different source types. Good support for users with screen readers.	Mendeley has better options for working with pdfs. No mobile app.
Endnote	Basic version is free with discount for students purchasing the full version.	Very customizable, with thousands of referencing styles available. Import citations and store pdfs.	Isn't as user-friendly as other managers and cannot extract citations from pdfs. Requires the user to be online to sync multiple devices.
Mendeley	Free for limited storage, with further paid premium options available.	Can store, highlight and annotate pdfs, as well as perform full-text-searches in pdfs. Android and iOS mobile app available.	Few accessibility features and support for users with screen readers.

Table 17   Software recommendations to help you manage your references

Each institution has its own policies on what constitutes plagiarism and the consequences of committing plagiarism and I strongly encourage you to look up your own institution's regulations. Aside from being aware of the rules, knowing how to properly use a referencing system to cite and reference external evidence will prevent the possibility of making any easily avoidable mistakes. Finally, using a reference manager will act as a safety net to help you catch missing or incomplete referencing information and will keep your (probably many!) sources nicely organized.

Next steps

	Find the rules on plagiarism for your institution (they should be on their website)
	Find out what referencing system you should be using in your research project
	Try out a couple of different reference managers and decide on which one you will use for your report
	Ask your supervisor if you have any questions about referencing or plagiarism

Exercise 5: Answers

1. *Which of the examples would be considered plagiarism, and why?*
   Example A is plagiarism. There are many similarities between the original and the example. In fact, the example simply rewords and replicates the structure of the original.

2. *Which of the examples do you think demonstrates the best understanding of the original, and why?*
   Example B shows the best understanding of the original. The writer of Example B discusses key points of the original in their own words. This shows that they understand the meaning of the information, not just how to make the information sound good.

3. *Which of the citations is correct?*
   The citation in Example B is correct and follows the Harvard system of referencing.

4. *Why didn't Example B use the numerical data given in the original?*
   It wasn't needed to make the point that the technique can differentiate between different food types.

Remember, there are many ways of paraphrasing an original source and, in this case, elements of information (not the wording) from the original have been used to make a new statement about the analytical technique used.

Exercise 6: Answers

1. *Which of the examples would be considered plagiarism, and why?*
   Example A is incorrect. The way this writer incorporates the evidence into a statement using a quote would be considered plagiarism because the quotation marks are incomplete (they are at the beginning of the quote, but are missing from the end), and the citation is placed at the end of the paragraph instead of directly after the quote itself.

2. *Why would the original be quoted instead of paraphrased?*
   The original is an official policy. The wording has been carefully chosen by the World Health Organisation for clarity to the reader. If the information is paraphrased, this might change how the meaning is interpreted, especially when it comes to a close analysis of the policy wording.

3. *Would it be appropriate in either example to use ellipses to remove some words or phrases?*
   No. All of the information in the original is relevant and should be included in the quote.

Editing and proofreading

Introduction

The final hurdle of the research journey is editing and proofreading your writing. This last stage is an essential part of science writing, and yet is one that many students don't fully complete. A thorough, systematic editing and proofreading process will ensure that you hand in the absolute best-quality work that you can. Properly executed editing can, in some cases, lift your potential mark by a whole grade boundary by eliminating simple errors of accuracy or omission. Editing and proofreading takes time, so build this in to your dissertation plan right at the beginning of the research process (see Chapter 4, Planning your work). The amount of time it will take to edit will, of course, vary between projects, but as a general guide, allow a day for each step in the process (up to six days for a dissertation) so that there is an adequate break built in between reading and re-reading your work.

Topics included in this chapter are:

- Editing your chapters as you write
- Editing your report as one document
- Handing your work in.

Editing task	How long might this take?	Completed
Chapter edit	A couple of hours	
Create one document	Half an hour	
Structural edit	A day or two	
Style edit	Four to six hours	
Copyedit	Three to four hours	
Proofreading	An hour or two	

Table 18 The editing checklist

Some tips for effective editing

Read aloud
You process writing differently when you read it aloud, so you're more likely to spot your own mistake if you read your work to yourself.

Take a break between writing and editing
You'll likely be sick of the sight of your own work and be less likely to see errors without a break.

Enlist some help!
Pick someone who doesn't know about your subject so that they focus on the quality of your writing, rather than the content of your work.

Print out your document
It's often easier to focus on close reading and navigate large documents on paper.

Be aware of your own bad habits!
Everyone has their own bad writing habits. Know yours and look out for them in your work.

The editing process: from beginning to end

1. Chapter editing
- Complete after you finish each chapter
- Check your chapter against your original plan
- Edit to add any missing information
- Check your writing flows logically

2. Create one document
- Do this after all draft chapters are written
- Place all individual chapters into one file
- Add title page, acknowledgements, abstract, contents pages
- Add bibliography and appendices

3. Structural editing
- Completed once you have a single document
- Check that the chapters are appropriately linked
- Check for inconsistencies between chapters
- Add signposting between chapters

4. Style editing
- Check you have used the correct academic tone
- Check that your arguments are complete and valid
- Check the clarity and concision of your writing
- Check that your writing is focused

5. Copy editing
- Correct any remaining technical issues with your writing
- Complete a spelling/grammar/punctuation check
- Check writing tense and terminology
- Typeset your dissertation

6. Proofreading
- To confirm your dissertation is ready (not make large changes)
- Read through the entire document
- Correct any minor text errors
- Correct any minor formatting errors

Chapter editing

The initial editing tasks should be completed as you finish each chapter of your dissertation. This means that when you pull together the individual chapters into one coherent document that will become your dissertation, you have already done the important work of editing the content of your writing while the chapter is still fresh in your head.

When completing chapter edits, it helps to work closely with your initial writing plan and the marking scheme, using these as a reference to guide your editing. Your chapter plan should ideally be bullet pointed under the planned section headings (see Chapter 8, page 121 for advice on planning a chapter). The first editing task to complete is to check through the plan and make sure that you have added all of the elements that you intended to. This includes all of the information and detail that your reader requires to understand your topic and research, and all of the academic literature that you wish to discuss. Double-checking your facts and figures is also a crucial task in chapter editing. Make sure that what you have said is right. At this point, add in or correct any missing/incorrect information where it is needed.

Use Figure 11 to check that each chapter of your dissertation includes all of the essential elements:

Introduction
- ✓ Provides initial background information
- ✓ Identifies the purpose of the research
- ✓ Gives an overview of your dissertation

Literature review
- ✓ All relevant topics are discussed
- ✓ All relevant literature are discussed
- ✓ Use the literature to identify the problem/gap

Method
- ✓ Includes all the detail required for your research to be replicable

Results
- ✓ All data has been reported in its raw form
- ✓ Summary of the data in writing

Discussion
- ✓ Use your data and the literature to answer your research question/s
- ✓ Discussion of the quality/significance of your data
- ✓ Include and discuss conflicting data
- ✓ Identify the limitations of the data/research

Conclusion
- ✓ Summary of the research
- ✓ The answer to your research question
- ✓ Recommendations based on your research

Figure 11 A checklist of the essential elements of a report or dissertation

Once you have made sure that you have covered all of the essential elements of the chapter you're editing, you should check your facts and arguments to make sure they are complete and correct. Any claim that you make should be backed up with evidence (either from the literature or from your own data). If you are unsure of any of the facts you have written about, go back and double-check the details. It's far easier to correct factual errors at this point – right at the beginning of the editing process – than it will be later on because factual corrections sometimes require an element of rewriting. Things to look out for are:

- Errors in reporting data
- Errors in statistical or mathematical equations
- Chronological errors
- Missing or inappropriate citations
- Errors in logic (i.e. your argumentation).

Complete chapter edits before you send any work to your supervisor. This means that you are sending the best version of your work possible, and your supervisor can focus on giving feedback on things that you wouldn't have ordinarily spotted by yourself. Of course, you will also very likely spot spelling and grammar errors during your chapter editing. Correct anything that you spot, but don't make searching for these more detailed errors a focus of your editing at this point. The purpose of the chapter edits are to make sure you have the content present and correct. Smaller, more technical errors are covered later in the editing process.

Create one document

To keep your dissertation writing organized, it helps to write each chapter in a separate document and save it as an individual file. That file can then be stored in a folder that is dedicated to that chapter, along with any notes, journal articles, data files and statistical models that you might produce for each chapter. Once the chapters of your dissertation have been written and edited in the way described above, the dissertation can be pulled together into one new document. Copy and paste each one of your chapters into a blank document that will form your finished dissertation. To this document you should add the following (see Chapter 8 for advice on constructing these individual elements):

1. Title page
2. Acknowledgements
3. Abstract

4. Table of contents
5. List of figures
6. List of tables

At the end of the document, insert your bibliography, ideally using your preferred reference manager (see Chapter 9 for advice on using reference managers). One of the most important editing checks to do at this point is to make sure that your references and citations are all present and correct. Even if you have used a reference manager, these aren't infallible. Check that each citation has a corresponding reference and that each entry in the bibliography has an associated citation. Finally, check that the format of your citations and bibliography match the system you have chosen to employ for your dissertation. This part of editing is long and boring, but absolutely essential to avoid accidental plagiarism.

Once you have one complete document with all of the chapters and bookends included, read through the whole dissertation once. At this point your work will seem somewhat fragmentary and disjointed, but that is normal. The reason for reading through the full report before you begin the more substantial edits is to get a sense of what the work reads like as one complete document. You'll find editing easier if you're not trying to remember later chapters in order to decide whether earlier ones are complete.

Editing the full dissertation

There are three stages of editing to work through before you hand in your dissertation: structural editing, style editing and copyediting. Each stage has a different function. Work through each stage in the order described here.

Stage 1: Structural edit

The first stage of editing your dissertation is a structural edit. This is a substantial editing task that will result in a lot of changes to your dissertation as you work through it. Through this edit you will refine the structure of your arguments, as well as the overall flow of your writing.

In order for your dissertation to read as one, coherent and flowing document, the first task of structural editing looks at how well the individual chapters of your work are linked together.

1. Begin the structural edit by reading the last paragraph of the introduction (first chapter) and the first paragraph of the second chapter (usually the literature review). Examine how well the introduction leads in the second chapter and think about whether a

transition sentence or paragraph is required. Repeat this step to link each of your chapters. Transition statements can link chapters by looking backward or forwards. Two examples are:
  a. In the next chapter, X, Y and Z will be discussed.
  b. As can be seen from the results, the data from the pilot study showed …

2. Add any necessary signposting required to link information between chapters. You'll notice that throughout this book, there are references to other chapters and pages in the volume; These references link topics and information without the need for repetition, ensuring that your reader has all of the information in a concise package. Where you see links between information in your dissertation, refer your reader to these by adding in some signposting.

3. Check that there are no details that you mention in earlier chapters that are subsequently missing in later ones. Pay particular attention to links between the literature review and the discussion for this one. If, for example, you argue in your literature review that the health effects of air pollution on young children is under-studied, your marker would expect to see this problem addressed in your discussion.

The second task of the structural edit looks at the flow of your writing to make sure that it makes sense. An effective exercise to complete to check the flow of your writing is 'reverse outlining'. The process for this exercise is as follows:

1. Identify the topic or main idea of each paragraph you have written.

2. If you cover multiple topics in one paragraph, consider whether you should break these into multiple paragraphs to ensure that your writing is properly structured (see Chapter 8 for advice on how to structure a paragraph).

3. Write a sentence that summarizes the topic/main idea of each paragraph. Number this list.

4. Check through your newly created outline and make changes in your report if appropriate:
  a. If you cover multiple topics in one paragraph, consider whether you should break these into multiple paragraphs in your report to ensure that your writing is properly structured.
  b. Does your outline make sense in the order that it is written, or do you need to swap some of your paragraphs around to achieve a better logical structure? If you swap any of your outline, think about how you should also swap these parts of your report.
  c. Are all of your sentences relevant to the point of your writing? Anything in your outline that deviates from your main topic or

argument should be edited out or moved to a different part of your report.

d. Is there any repetition of topics or ideas? If you spot two sentences in your outline that cover the same point, consider whether you explain the point clearly enough in your report, or whether you felt that you needed to revisit the topic to clarify yourself. You may wish to combine or remove paragraphs in your report that duplicate topics or ideas.

The structural edit can sometimes feel frustrating because it requires a bit of checking backwards and forwards through the chapters of your dissertation. If you skim read the results through (there's no need to read the whole dissertation again), you'll find that the quality of the whole document feels significantly improved compared to your initial read through. This is because you've knitted the once separate chapters into one complete report. You'll also be pleased to know that editing becomes a lot easier from here!

Stage 2: Style edit

The chapter edits and the structural edits should have resulted in a report that has all of the correct information presented in the correct order. The style edit that follows this focuses on how you write, rather than on what you write. Although there are lots of style principles in science writing that are pre-prescribed to you (e.g. the use of formal academic tone), there are some that you need to define yourself. It helps to decide on these principles before you begin the style edit, so that you have a guide to work with as you edit your dissertation.

If your institution doesn't have their own style guide (check their website and ask your supervisor) you may want to create your own guide as you write your dissertation. This means recording certain stylistic decisions that you make in a separate word document. This makes the job of defining your writing style much easier when it comes to editing. Whenever you make a decision in your writing that isn't already prescribed by the standard rules of English, make a note of it. Aspects of style that you might want to consider for your style guide include:

- Referencing system (e.g. APA or Chicago?)
- Punctuation (e.g. will you use single or double quotation marks where required?)
- Spelling (e.g. will you use standard English or American spelling?)
- Use of numbers (e.g. will you spell out numbers or use numerals?)

- Acronyms and abbreviations (e.g. will you use full stops with abbreviations – Ph.D versus PhD).
- Hyphenation of subject-specific terms (e.g. socioeconomic or socio-economic?)

There are several published academic style guides that are normally available through your institutions' library. The APA Style Manual and the Chicago Manual of Style are the two best known in science subjects. These can be useful to help you decide what sorts of stylistic decisions you should make; however, unless you have been specifically referred to these by your institution, don't use these guide to define the writing style of your dissertation. Published style guides are intended for use by writers and editors in professional academic publishing. Following a set guide that you are unfamiliar with can become unnecessarily complicated because, ultimately, it doesn't matter what style decisions you make, just as long as you are consistent in your style throughout your dissertation.

Defining and recording stylistic decisions, and then using these decisions as a style guide to edit your completed dissertation will result in a professional sounding and consistent piece of writing. As a result, your dissertation will be clearer, more accurately written and easier to mark. Don't worry about style decisions that are related to how the document looks at this point. Things like fonts, margins and heading styles are part of formatting, which comes right at the end of the editing process.

Stage 3: Copyedit

The next stage of editing is the copyedit. This is the last stage of editing where you might reasonably expect to be making changes to your paper. The purpose of the copyedit is to correct any minor technical errors; these might include spelling, grammar and punctuation errors, as well as correcting small errors in any figures and table you have. An important part of copyediting looks at your references and citations, and will ensure that you don't commit accidental plagiarism by missing out any vital information when referring to external sources. The final task of the copyedit is to typeset your document so that it looks polished and professional.

You may want to complete your copyedit by reading a printed version of your report or dissertation – catching small errors is potentially easier when reading from paper because research has shown that the working memory and the ability to focus is better when reading from paper compared to reading from a screen. Of course, you must also consider the environmental cost of printing out large documents, so it is a good idea to be confident that you have fully completed the previous editing steps and have run the relevant editor tools in your word processor before printing out your work for copyediting.

If you do decide to print your work out, you have the luxury of being able to edit your work wherever you choose, without the constraint of laptop batteries or desks. Take advantage of this and edit your work in a different location to where you wrote it. You'll be surprised how much the new surroundings refreshes your focus. When copyediting, closely read through the whole document and mark with a pen or highlighter any mistakes that you spot. Add in or cross out incorrect punctuation, write short notes in the margins and highlight any formatting inconsistencies you spot along the way. The amendments you make at this point should be very minor, so if you spot issues with paragraph structure or your scientific argument, take this as an indicator that you're not quite ready for copyediting.

Below is a checklist of things to look out for while copyediting:

1. Spelling, grammar and punctuation
   Spellcheck isn't infallible. Check particularly for words that are only incorrectly spelled in the context of the sentence (e.g. of vs. off, plane vs. plain, powder vs. power etc.). Also check that you are using the correct grammatical tense (past, present or future) and that you don't arbitrarily jump between them throughout your writing.

2. Page numbers and headers
   Document breaks within your report might throw off your page numbers, so make sure they are all present and correct. Also ensure that all headers and subheaders are a standard font, font size and indentation. The styles pane in Microsoft Word is useful here and will make your table of content easier to construct.

3. Technical terms and proper names
   Double-check that each instance of technical nomenclature is correct and the proper names are consistently capitalized.

4. Maths
   There is no need to re-run each statistical test from the beginning, but check that the outcome of each instance of maths that you come across (e.g. mean values, percentages, etc.) looks right. Only double-check the working of anything that seems 'off'.

5. Font size, line spacing, text alignment
   Make sure the body text of your work is a consistent font type and size. Check that there is consistent spacing between each line (usually 1.5 or double spaced for a report or dissertation) and that spacing between

paragraphs is also consistent. When aligning your text, justified text is usually the most polished option for your work. Double-check for lines where words are too squashed in or too spaced out, though; tidy these up with a soft line break or soft return (shift+enter).

6. References and citations
This one is rather a laborious task, but is absolutely essential; check that each citation in your text has an entry in your bibliography, then check that each entry in your bibliography has an in-text citation. This means that you won't have any missing or additional references in your bibliography. You can use the 'find' function in Microsoft Word to help with this (ctrl+f).

7. Cross-references
You will probably refer your reader back and forth through your report (e.g. 'see p. 5 for a description of volcanic lightning') and you will frequently refer to figures and table (e.g. 'see table 15'). All of your editing will have moved your text about a little as you add and delete small elements, so check each one of these references to make sure they still refer to the correct page number/item.

Proofreading

Proofreading is an exciting stage of the writing process because it is the last time you will see your work before submitting. Proofreading is also relatively simple because you are simply performing one complete read-through of the final version of your dissertation or report. It's really important to complete proofreading to catch any final, minor errors (and there will be some!) and to read your work as your marker will see it. There is no one focus for proofreading because you should look out for any type of error in your work. If you spot something that isn't right, this is your last chance to correct it! It can help to enlist a willing volunteer to help with proofreading since a fresh pair of eyes will be far more likely to identify corrections. A word of caution about involving third parties, though; avoid online 'proofreading' services that charge a fee – you can never guarantee their academic integrity and they can be unnecessarily expensive. It is best to ask a friend or family member who is unfamiliar with your subject to help with proofreading as they are more likely to focus on the quality of your writing instead of the factual content of your work (this avoids plagiarism by collusion). If you find a willing volunteer, ask them to mark up your work with comments or tracked changes (never ever any unmarked changes), and be prepared to buy them a bottle of something to say thank you. Of course, enlisting help with your proofreading doesn't mean that you don't have to also proofread your work yourself – treat it as an extra safety net only.

Conclusion

You'll have seen by now that there are several, in-depth stages to correctly editing a report or dissertation. Once you have completed them, though, you can be absolutely confident that you have produced the best possible version of your work. Congratulations! You can finally submit your work for assessment. Be sure to do one final check of any bound copies of your research – I have personal experience of having a dissertation bound upside down, which would have made reading and marking it quite a challenge! Above all, once you have submitted your work, take the time to relax and celebrate your achievement. You will likely have at some point thought that you would never finish your research, and you're also likely to miss working on it in the weeks to come. A carefully planned treat will give you the closure you will inevitably need. Good luck with your submission!

Glossary

Here is a list of specialist terms that are used in scientific research. You may come across these in journal papers, conversations with your supervisor, conferences, formal assessment instructions and anywhere else in the sphere of scientific research.

Accurate
Accuracy describes how close a measured point is to the true value. Data, observations and arguments are accurate if they correctly represent the facts.

Case study
A case study examines a real-world example of a chosen topic. Because a case study is so narrowly focused, researchers are able to go into in-depth detail when describing and analysing the example.

Case-control study
A case-control study is a clinical study that observes two groups of people – one with a medical condition and one without. There are no interventions in a case-control study, instead researchers examine the participants' medical histories and lifestyles to make a causal connection between a person's history and their condition.

Cohort study
A cohort study follows a defined group of people over time. Measurements and observations from the group (cohort) are compared over time, usually to test the effect of an intervention or environmental factor/s.

Consultation
A discussion with people from the population that the research is intended to impact (e.g. public, patients, employees, students) to help make decisions about how the research should be conducted. Consultation can be in many forms, e.g. survey, forum, focus group, poll, etc.

Control
Controls help researchers establish a causal relationship. Data is collected from a control sample-set or control group of participants that have not been subjected to the experimental intervention.

Dissemination
How research is communicated. Research can be disseminated in many forms (written reports, oral presentations, podcasts, posters) and to many audiences (the public, other academics in your field, academics outside your subject).

Editorial (in an academic journal)
An editorial is usually written by a member of the editorial team in a journal and is akin to an opinion piece on a particular subject. Editorials are commonly used to introduce special issues of a journal (issues comprising papers that all that focus on one topic). They have the same academic strength as scientific evidence as expert opinion (see next entry).

Expert opinion	An expert opinion can be given to you in person (by a lecturer, for example) or can be published in writing in a journal. Usually, these opinions are considered as informed viewpoints. They are the comments of someone who is an authority in their field, but their comments aren't necessarily accompanied by objective evidence. You might want to use expert opinion to back up an argument in your research but consider its strength as academic evidence.
Exponential increase/decrease	The word 'exponential' is often misused to mean that something is happening quickly. In fact, an exponential increase or decrease in maths means that the speed of the change is proportional to the size of the population. If that relationship between growth/decay and the population cannot be established, then it is not exponential.
Focus group	A means of generating qualitative data, a focus group is an invited panel of six to ten people who are brought together to discuss a particular topic. Focus group discussions can be quite loose and open or can be more directed, and the conversation is usually recorded for later analysis by the researcher.
Grey literature	Any literature that is produced by a reputable source (e.g. a university research group) but is not published by an official academic or commercial publisher is called grey literature. Examples of grey literature include unpublished lab reports, government documents and dissertations.
Hypothesis	A hypothesis is an informed, academic guess at the outcome of your research. It is what you expect to see, given your current knowledge of the subject. In inferential statistics, it is common to state a null hypothesis (which assumes no relationship between two variables/sets of variables and is usually the commonly accepted view) and an alternative hypothesis (the opposite of the null hypothesis).
Intervention	Usually found in medical, veterinary and other life sciences, an intervention is something intended to make a positive change (e.g. a drug, lifestyle programme, environmental change) and is usually the concept that is being tested in scientific research.
Methodology	Different to your research method, methodology is the process you go through when evaluating potential ways to investigate your research question and choosing the best method for your project.
Multidisciplinary research	Research that investigates a research question using tools from more than one academic field is multidisciplinary. If you are conducting multidisciplinary research, it is beneficial to have a supervisor from each discipline to advise you.

Multi-methodological research	A project that uses more than one approach to answer the research questions is multi-methodological. The methods used might be from the same academic field or might be from more than one field (the latter would also be multidisciplinary research). Multi-methodological research is arguably better quality than single-method research because matching conclusions drawn from the independent approaches can corroborate each other.
Peer review	All (credible) journal articles are subject to peer review before publication. This means that a group of academics who are experts on the topic of the proposed paper critically analyse the work and make a recommendation about its suitability for publication.
Pilot study	A pilot study is sometimes carried out before a large-scale piece of research begins. It usually includes fewer measurements/samples/participants than the planned larger project and the results of a pilot study can be used to determine whether a particular line of enquiry is worth pursuing and if the chosen method is appropriate for the research.
Placebo	Usually in medicine, a placebo is an intervention that has no effect on the patient. Placebos are used to test whether the trialled intervention is effective, or if a person responds to treatment simply because they believe they are being treated (called the placebo effect).
Precise	Precision describes how close repeated measurements of the same observation are to each other. Precise repeated measurements of a sample will result in the same result each time, even if that result is not the true value (i.e. accurate).
Protocol	Another term for research method. A detailed written plan of how you conducted your research, including information about the materials, samples, participants and/or equipment used.
Qualitative research	Research that collects and analyses non-numerical data (such as spoken words, survey results, observations of natural phenomena, etc.) to investigate a research topic. Qualitative research commonly aims to give an in-depth understanding of the chosen topic, rather than to prove or disprove a hypothesis.
Quality control indicator	A quality control indicator, especially in Analytical Chemistry, is a range of acceptable values that are usually calculated from a huge amount of individual measurements of known quality samples. If an unknown sample falls outside this range, the quality of the sample (e.g. the state of preservation) can be assumed to be poor and the data should be discarded.

Quantitative research	Research that measures, records and analyses numerical data is quantitative. Quantitative research usually tests a hypothesis and includes statistical analysis of the data.
Randomized control trial	Common in clinical subjects, two cohorts are observed – an experimental group and a control group. The decision about which group the participants are assigned to is made at random by a computer programme so that potential bias is eliminated.
Scoping review	A scoping review aims to find out how much literature there is on a given topic to inform us about the state of the art and gaps in the knowledge, and therefore make recommendations about future research directions. These can be standalone journal papers or a small part of a larger project. The literature review in your research report is a type of scoping review.
Statistically significant	When researchers say that something is statistically significant, they mean that it is mathematically probable that an observed relationship is not due to chance. Be careful when using the word 'significant' in scientific research, as readers might assume that you are referring to statistical significance – even if you are not.
Systematic review	A systematic review is a type of literature review that has a very carefully defined method for searching for, including and excluding and analysing literature on a topic.
Thesis (referring to a report)	A written report of research – another name for a dissertation or a research report.
Thesis (referring to a statement)	An idea or theory that the producer intends to prove in their research.
Viva	A viva is an oral exam that is usually associated with a PhD qualification but can also be required for other degrees. A viva is usually led by a panel of academics who have read a student's research and have questions about the work's credibility, originality and applicability.

Further reading

Boyle, Jennifer and Scott Ramsay (2023) *Writing for Science Students*. London: Bloomsbury.

Cite them right. www.citethemrightonline.com.

Copus, Julia (2009) *Brilliant Writing Tips for Students* (Pocket Study Skills). London: Bloomsbury.

Greetham, Bryan (2021) *How to Write Your Literature Review*. London: Bloomsbury.

Joseph, Kate and Chris Irons (2018) *Managing Stress* (Pocket Study Skills). London: Bloomsbury.

Leedy, Paul and Jeanne Ellis Ormrod (2015) *Practical Research: Planning and Design*. Harlow: Pearson.

Martin, Andrew and Andrew Elliot (2016) 'The role of personal best (PB) goal setting in students' academic achievement gains', *Learning and Individual Differences*, 45: 222–7.

Neville, Colin (2010) *The Complete Guide to Guide to Referencing and Avoiding Plagiarism*. London: Open University Press.

Pears, Richard and Graham Shields (2022) *Cite Them Right – The Essential Referencing Guide*. London: Bloomsbury.

Wellington, Jerry (2010) *Making Supervision Work for You: A Student's Guide*. London: SAGE.*

Williams, Kate (2021) *Getting Critical* (Pocket Study Skills). London: Bloomsbury.

Williams, Kate (2018) *Planning Your Dissertation* (Pocket Study Skills). London: Bloomsbury.

Williams, Kate and Michelle Reid (2011) *Time Management* (Pocket Study Skills). London: Bloomsbury.

Zozus, Meredith (2018) *The Data Book: Collection and Management of Research Data*. Boca Raton, FL: CRC Press.

---

* Although this book is aimed at PhD students, it gives a really good insight to effective and productive student–supervisor relationships.

Index

Numbers in **bold** refer to pages with key or in-depth information on a topic.